ALSO BY RUTH ADAMS BRONZ

❋

MISS RUBY'S AMERICAN COOKING:
From Border to Border & Coast to Coast,
the Best Recipes
from America's Regional Kitchens

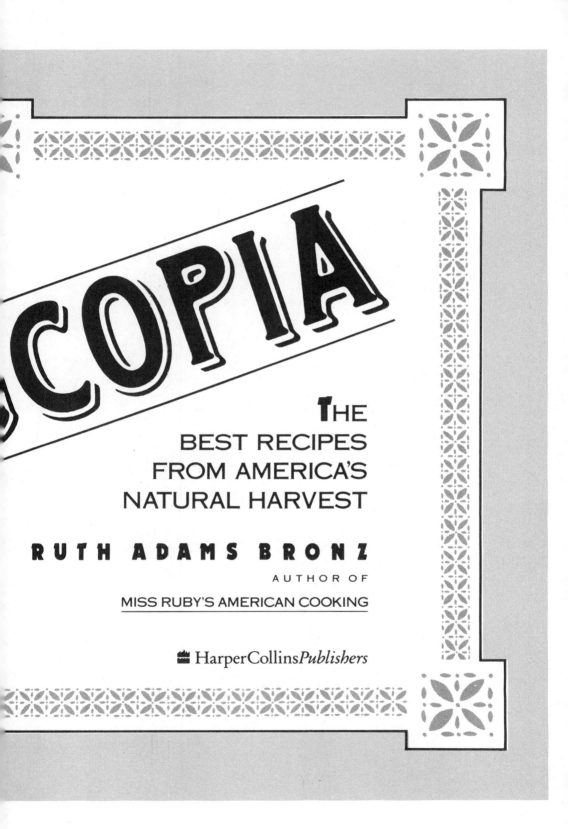

COPIA

THE
BEST RECIPES
FROM AMERICA'S
NATURAL HARVEST

RUTH ADAMS BRONZ

AUTHOR OF

MISS RUBY'S AMERICAN COOKING

HarperCollins*Publishers*

FIRST EDITION

DESIGNED BY JOEL AVIROM

Library of Congress Cataloging-in-Publication Data

Bronz, Ruth Adams.
  Miss Ruby's cornucopia: the best recipes from America's natural harvest/Ruth
Adams Bronz.
     p.   cm.
  ISBN 0-06-016204-X (cloth)
  1. Cookery, American.   I. Title
  TX715.B8491347   1991   90-55527
  641.5973—dc20

     91   92   93   94   95   CC/RRD   10   9   8   7   6   5   4   3   2   1

To Michael Dorsey,
who lived through all of it, liked most of it,
and never stopped talking to me

CONTENTS

ACKNOWLEDGMENTS

IN PERFORMING ARTS, the debts are always enormous and the thanks endless. I'm especially grateful to cooks who read my recipes and shared theirs, eaters who gave opinions of finished dishes, and fellow workers who tested, retested, and revised to come up with finished products we were all happy with. At Miss Ruby's, Charles Kahlstrom and Paula Frazier have been constant sources of encouragement and support and have devised recipes, tested and commented on them. They never flagged.

Traditional American cooking has limits different from those of the recipes in this book, some of which I invented, some of which I adapted from the work of other cooks, and some of which *are* the work of other cooks. This is in the nature of any collaborative art, and cooking is perhaps the most collaborative of all arts. I hope I've given all credit where it is due; I owe more than I can say, beginning with my remotest ancestor and coming down to the cooks I worked with this morning.

ADORED, DEVOURED, AND UNCONSIDERED

AMERICAN COOKING IS VARIOUS in its ingredients and in its techniques. We enjoy it voraciously but whether we'll ever recognize what it is remains to be seen. We found when we got here a wealth of raw materials never seen in the Old World, and we applied old traditions to them with invention and gusto. For the first 150 years we were a nation of farmers, producing a broad abundance of fresh materials, and generations of women who cooked three meals a day for hungry families who loved to eat. When the Industrial Revolution hit and a lot of us ended up in big cities, we traded among ourselves the cooking traditions we brought with us as immigrants. But the neglect of our cooking may have begun here too: It's been said that our melting pot was really an Anglo-conformist pot, that for years we didn't come together in all our diversity but just tried to aspire to the dominant English culture. And the dominant English food, too.

So we went on eating pasta and collard greens and tabbouleh and caldo verde, but we hardly realized it. We *believed* that all we ate was roast beef and mashed potatoes and cabbage—all that other stuff tasted good, but didn't count. (I have a friend from the South Side of Chicago who never heard the word "sauce" when he was growing up—his family was Italian and they ate a lot of pasta, but the red tomato stuff they put on it was always called "gravy." This is America; Americans eat gravy, but do you think we're really going to give up marinara?)

The result of all this variety in our backgrounds and our kitchens and all this conformity to an Anglo ideal in our heads is a wonderful kitchen virtually ignored, but never deserted, and a whole range of raw materials turned into wonderful dishes, eaten voraciously all over the country and almost never thought of as cooking at all. Corn is probably the best example: I once did a corn menu based partly on my long apprenticeship in regional American cooking and partly on the research of Betty Fussell, who is writing a book on corn. It had a variety and interest that most menus based on one ingredient could never have, partly because of the remarkable properties of corn—it is a sugar, a starch, a vegetable, and, in combination with beans, a complete protein—and partly because we've made such ingenious and broad use of it. We have recipes for puddings, scallops, spoon breads, corn breads, tamales, enchiladas, posole, chowders, and even ice cream, all made of corn and all tasting so different from one another that it's hard to believe that they have any ingredient in common. But when I talked to people about the menu before I did it, they said, "Well, what are you going to do after corn on the cob?"

Considering that the questioners were all Americans raised on all those wonderful corn dishes of which I could only number a bare few in my menu, it struck me as a very odd reaction. But then I realized that corn is a native American ingredient, adopted by us immigrants and eaten for our whole history, but having no place in the traditional European and Asian cultures. Apart from polenta in Italy, it isn't eaten at all in Western Europe; imported from the New World, it was immediately seen as horse fodder, and that's how it's been used ever since.

Most Europeans have never even tasted, and cannot imagine, the recent and luscious hybrids of sweet corn that make it such a delicacy. And public eating in America, the restaurant and ceremonial eating that we identify with, is European. What we eat at home has until recently had no place in our public life, and so doesn't exist at the conscious level, at least officially. We don't see corn or sweet potatoes or blueberries or chiles or cranberries as food, formally. They are just what we eat, quotidian and ordinary and never in some important way seeing the public light of day. Great chefs have ignored them; diners-out of distinction never refer to them, don't miss them in their favorite restaurants; and their presence on a menu outside private houses is seen to bring the level of the whole event down a peg.

Until recently. Now, and a little disconcertingly, a whole generation of French-trained American professional cooks are beginning to discover American ingredients, though in a fairly timid and derivative way: It doesn't seem a great triumph for American cooking to flavor a hollandaise sauce with cranberry purée. So far, American recipes for the great American ingredients are still being ignored in the most ambitious professional circles, so that more sophisticated refinements on them aren't being explored yet. Except of course at Miss Ruby's Cafe, where we've been concentrating on American ingredients and American recipes for years. We're devoted to the traditional uses of traditional ingredients, but having been at it for ten years or so, we find ourselves beginning to play our own changes. You'll find some of them in this book, along with many older recipes—you'll recognize them, you were raised on them—in a tribute to the broad abundance of raw materials and finished dishes that were all born in the U.S.A.

CRANBERRIES

The cranberry is dark red, deeply acidic, and so full of pectin that it practically seizes up as it's cooked—you don't even have to wait for it to cool. It doesn't lose its color when it's heated, it can be used to acidify and tint almost anything, and sweetened, it can produce dishes from sweet-and-sour sauces to rich and colorful desserts.

Absolutely indigenous—there are four or five Indian names for it —it was used by Native Americans as a poultice for wounds. When the white settler arrived, he adopted the cranberry almost at once, as he did corn, and cultivated it widely if not intensively. Grown through the high summer, it is harvested in early September in time for the holidays it has graced since the European arrived. Its natural habitat was fully exploited in the mid-nineteenth century in Cape Cod with the development of the cranberry bog. Making use of the low-lying, floodable salt marshes of the area, cultivators also broadcast sand over the developing plants to encourage fruit production. Flooding creates an effective and elegant method of harvesting—eggbeater-like pickers (which have replaced the earlier cranberry scoops) are driven through watery fields to pluck off the cranberries, which ride on the water's surface in a great red tide. They are then seined up and later bounced to determine good condition (nine bounces is an indication of a really fresh cranberry). In flavor, color, and cultivation, there is nothing quite like it.

Until recently, the cranberry met the same fate as a lot of American foods with no handy European equivalents. Quickly taken up for relishes and the kind of sweet-and-sour sauce designed to accompany, rather than be served on, large pieces of meat, the settlers made cranberries at once accepted and ignored. When Thanksgiving and Christmas, with their dishes of jelled and whole-berry sauces, were past, no one thought of cranberries for the rest of the year. Bright, acid, and emphatic in flavor, they had no place in the blandness of English cooking; and later, when Americans began to take an interest in French and Italian food, it was obvious that the cranberry didn't fit into the scheme of either cuisine.

Even the discovery by Ocean Spray that it could sell millions of gallons of cranberry juice cocktail hasn't seemed to encourage cooks to a broader use of this remarkable fruit—possibly because, like rhubarb, it's so sour that it has to be used judiciously to acidify or to be heavily sweetened as a fruit for desserts. It's just not possible to pop a cranberry into your mouth and eat it.

As usual with even our most neglected foods, though, some cooks have worked out recipes worthy of such an intense and colorful fruit —onward from Thanksgiving!

SOME BASICS

⬚

Cranberries are easy to use because they're bright, intense in color and flavor, and so full of pectin that no matter what you use them for, you never have to worry about a thin preparation. But they have one drawback that discourages cooks—they are dead sour, the kind of sour that turns the mouth inside out and curls the toes. The best antidote to this is to develop a simple formula for sweetening them that will let you reach into the refrigerator and pull them out as you would any other fruit.

Basic Sweetened Cranberries

MAKES 2 CUPS

1 pound cranberries, washed and picked over

1½ cups sugar

Simmer the cranberries and sugar in a 1-quart nonreactive sauce-pan just until the cranberries begin to pop, about 15 minutes. Use as is as cranberry sauce, or store for future use, up to 6 weeks in the refrigerator or a year in the freezer.

Frozen Cranberries

Fresh cranberries are available in the early and late fall, right up to Christmastime, and frozen cranberries can be had all year, but not in very steady or reliable supply. So if you like cranberries as much as I do and want to be able to use them at will, freeze a few pounds when you can find them.

Pour a pound or more of fresh cranberries in one layer onto a sided cookie sheet. Freeze. Pour into plastic bags and store in the freezer for up to a year.

Cranberry Purée

MAKES 2½ CUPS

If you want the color and flavor of cranberries without the bulk of the whole fruit, you can reduce cranberries to a purée that will also serve to thicken other preparations.

1 pound cranberries, washed and picked over	*1½ cups sugar* *½ cup water*

Simmer ingredients until cranberries have fallen apart, about 45 minutes. Add another ½ cup water if the mixture is too thick to stir easily with a wooden spoon. Purée in a food processor until very smooth, about 4 minutes. Pass through a chinoise or fine-mesh sieve and refrigerate or freeze.

RELISHES AND SAUCES

Raw Cranberry-Orange Relish

MAKES 3 CUPS

This is the one I'd keep if I had to give up all the other cranberry sauces I know—I've tried to steer away from it, but recent Thanksgivings have seen it on the table by the quart. It improves with age up to three days, and will often keep longer. It is wonderful on the the traditional day-after sandwich, with turkey, a little mayonnaise, and good white bread, and terrific by itself on pumpernickel.

1 pound cranberries, washed
and picked over
1 whole thin-skinned orange,
seeded and cut into 2-inch
chunks

1½ cups sugar
½ cup Cointreau

Put all the ingredients in a food processor bowl and turn on and off until you've got a rough purée—do not overprocess. Or use an old-fashioned meat grinder—it works very well. (A blender tends to purée the ingredients too fine.) Let stand at least 2 hours to marry the flavors.

Cranberry Chutney

MAKES 6 CUPS

This is a spicy, apple-y chutney, very good with fresh or smoked pork, and surprisingly satisfying with beef. Like many chutneys, it's also great on Cheddar cheese sandwiches.

2 cups cranberries, chopped
   fine
10 tart apples, pared, cored,
   and chopped fine
3 green bell peppers, chopped
   fine

1 cup raisins
1 cup cider vinegar
1 cup dark brown sugar
¼ cup grated fresh ginger
2 teaspoons cayenne
1 teaspoon ground allspice

You may chop cranberries, apples, and peppers together in the bowl of a food processor, but take care they remain in a fine dice and are not reduced to a purée—use about 5 turns of the blade at first, then check the results.

Mix all ingredients well and simmer over low heat, stirring frequently, until thickened, 30 or 40 minutes. Pour into sterilized jars and seal, or store in an earthenware crock in the refrigerator.

Cranberry-Walnut Sauce with a Zing

MAKES 4 CUPS

1 pound cranberries, washed
  and picked over
1 cup sugar

½ cup prepared horseradish
1 cup fine-chopped walnuts
1 cup sour cream (optional)

Simmer cranberries and sugar together in a 1-quart nonreactive saucepan until cranberries have popped and are about to fall apart. Cool, then stir in horseradish and walnuts. Chill until ready to use.

For a smoother, richer sauce, add the sour cream just before serving.

Cooked Orange-Cranberry Sauce

MAKES 2½ CUPS

1 pound cranberries, washed
   and picked over
1 orange, zest grated and
   pulp chopped fine

1½ cups sugar
½ cup Cointreau
¼ teaspoon ground cloves

Simmer everything together in a 1-quart nonreactive saucepan until the berries are tender and just popping, about 30 minutes, stirring from the bottom every 10 minutes or so. Cool to room temperature, then chill until ready to use.

MAIN DISHES

⁂

Grilled Salmon with Cranberry Glaze

SERVES 6

Salmon is a wonderful fish with some strange affinities. It goes beautifully with red wine; in spite of its oil-richness, it is lovely with hollandaise sauce and mayonnaise, and it tastes wonderful with fruit —I use raspberry purée and raspberry vinegar with it frequently and am very fond of this recipe, which is, of course, a variation on a classic.

3 tablespoons Cranberry Puree (page 8)	6 salmon steaks, about 8 ounces each
1 tablespoon red wine vinegar	1 cup whole cranberries,
2 tablespoons extra-fine sugar	poached in 1 cup water
1 cup red Bordeaux	with ½ cup sugar

To make the glaze, heat cranberry purée, vinegar, and sugar together until sugar melts. Add wine and simmer for 10 minutes.

Light charcoal in the grill and wait for the coals to turn gray; about 20 minutes. Over a very low flame, melt ¼ pound butter. Skim residue from the surface, then pour the clear yellow liquid out into a deep platter, leaving behind the milky solids. Dip salmon steaks in the clarified butter and grill at closest setting to the coals, about 3 minutes on each side (they should be just translucent at the center). Serve on a pool of the glaze, brushed with additional glaze and garnished with the whole sweetened cranberries and watercress.

These go wonderfully, if oddly, with turned, boiled, and sautéed sweet potatoes.

Smothered Rabbit with Mustard Greens and Cathy Casey's Cranberry-Sage Vinaigrette

SERVES 4

This is the simplest of meat recipes, with a lot of complex flavors as background: the peppery mustard greens and the sour/sweet/sagey excitement of the vinaigrette. Cathy is a chef who always takes advantage of all the flavors of her region, a lot of them inherited from the Dust Bowl refugees who headed west in the thirties.

*2 rabbits, about 3 pounds
   each
2 cups flour, seasoned with
   salt and pepper
8 slices bacon, diced
2 cups dry white wine (a
   Muscadet is fine)
3 cups chicken stock
6 cups young mustard greens,
   washed, dried, and torn as
   for salad*

*⅔ cup Cranberry-Sage
   Vinaigrette (see following
   recipe)
4 cups cooked wild and white
   rice, mixed
Watercress sprigs and Basic
   Sweetened Cranberries
   (page 7) for garnish*

Cut rabbit into saddle and hindquarter pieces, bone in. Preheat oven to 425° F.

Dredge rabbit pieces in flour and lay out one layer deep in a lightly greased roasting pan. Render bacon and pour fat over the rabbit; reserve pieces of bacon. Roast rabbit, turning once halfway through the cooking time, until rich brown on all sides, about 40 minutes. When rabbit is brown, add white wine and 1 cup of the stock to the pan and cover tightly with foil. Reduce oven heat to 350 ° F and cook until rabbit is very tender, about 1 hour longer.

When rabbit is done, toss mustard greens with vinaigrette and lay in an oval in the middle of an oval platter. Arrange the rabbit pieces around the outside of the oval, overlapping the mustard greens.

Scrape the bottom of the rabbit pan and add a cup of chicken stock to deglaze the pan. Simmer briefly, then strain the pan juices and skim. Pour over the rabbit and sprinkle with whole sweetened cranberries and the browned pieces of diced bacon. Garnish with watercress sprigs. Serve at once, accompanied by mixed wild and brown rices.

Cranberry-Sage Vinaigrette

1 package (12 ounces)
   cranberries
1½ cups orange juice
½ cup sugar
½ cup Dijon mustard
¾ cup honey
1¼ cups champagne vinegar
   or white wine vinegar

1 cup soy oil
½ cup walnut oil
2 tablespoons fine-chopped
   fresh sage
¼ cup fine-chopped shallots
Salt and pepper to taste

Cook cranberries, orange juice, and sugar in a nonreactive saucepan over medium heat until cranberries pop. Cool. Purée cranberry mixture and set aside. In a mixing bowl, mix mustard and honey, and whip in vinegar, cranberry mixture, and oil, a little at a time, until emulsified. Add sage and shallots; season with salt and pepper.

Shaker Cranberry Pot Roast

SERVES 6

This is perhaps the perfect winter dish—hearty but bright enough to cheer up a gray day.

5 pounds bottom round roast
Salt and pepper
1 cup flour
½ pound suet
2 large onions, quartered and
    sliced

3 cloves
1 bay leaf
6 cups beef stock
2 cups raw cranberries,
    washed and picked over
⅔ cup sugar

Rub roast with salt, pepper, and flour; render suet in a 4-quart Dutch oven or a heavy, covered roasting pan and remove browned pieces. Brown roast all over in fat and remove from pot. Remove all but 2 tablespoons of fat from the pot and add onions, stirring until beige. Return roast to pot along with cloves, bay leaf, and beef stock. Cover and simmer or oven-cook for 3 hours, or until fork-tender. Thirty minutes before the roast is done, add the cranberries and sugar to the liquid in the pot.

When beef is done, remove from pot and set aside in a warm place. Drain the pot juices and reserve the cranberries and onions, removing bay leaf and cloves. Skim the pot juices and return to the fire, boiling over a medium flame to reduce by half. Return the cranberries and onions to juices, stir to combine, and serve as a sauce over the sliced pot roast.

If you want to make it a one-pot meal, cut 2 pounds of a variety of the sweeter roots—rutabaga, parsnips, carrots, and sweet potatoes—into 2-inch chunks and add them to the pot juices an hour before the roast is done. Otherwise, serve with baked or mashed sweet potatoes. Wonderful, too, with cranberry muffins or blueberry muffins instead of bread.

OTHER GOOD THINGS

Cranberry Muffins

MAKES ABOUT 1 DOZEN
MEDIUM-SIZE MUFFINS

Cranberry muffins, like blueberry muffins, are part of the quick-bread, fruit-bread tradition that's uniquely American—slightly sweet loaves or muffins, baking-powder raised, and in some parts of the country eaten with main meals as well as at breakfast and between meals.

½ cup confectioners' sugar
¾ cup cranberries, coarsely
   chopped
2 cups flour
3 teaspoons baking powder

½ teaspoon salt
¼ cup sugar
1 egg, beaten
1 cup milk
4 tablespoons butter, melted

Preheat oven to 400° F.

Sprinkle confectioners' sugar over the cranberries and toss together. Set aside. Sift together flour, baking powder, salt, and sugar. Combine the egg, milk, and melted butter and add the dry ingredients until they are completely absorbed. Stir in the cranberries until they are completely blended. Spoon into greased and floured muffin tins, to about two-thirds full. Bake for 20 minutes, or until a knife blade comes out clean.

Cranberries and Winter Squash with Onions

SERVES 8

Cranberries are the perfect foil for the rich blandness of winter squash—and the colors are beautiful together.

1 Hubbard (or acorn or any
   yellow winter) squash,
   about 2 pounds, peeled,
   seeded, and cut into 2-inch
   chunks
1 large Spanish onion,
   minced

¼ pound butter
Salt and pepper to taste
2 teaspoons nutmeg
2 cups Basic Sweetened
   Cranberries (page 7)

Cover squash with boiling water and simmer until just tender. Meanwhile, sauté onion in butter until translucent; add salt and pepper and nutmeg. Drain squash, reserving 1 cup of the boiling water. Add squash and the water to onion. Simmer until water is all absorbed and squash is perfectly tender. Mash squash until it is fluffy. Put a scoop of squash on each plate, make an indentation in each, and top with a dollop of cranberries.

If you bake the squash with 2 cups of grated mild cheese—muenster or Bel Paese—and a sprinkle of Parmesan on top, you can serve it with the cranberry sauce as a light lunch dish. Just add a salad and toasted banana bread.

DESSERTS

Cranberry Ice

MAKES 4½ CUPS

This ice is a study in contrasts—light in texture, intense in color and flavor. Served with Concord grape ice on the same plate, it positively vibrates. I use it at lavish Thanksgiving dinners, to shock the palate before the richness of turkey.

4 cups raw cranberries, washed and picked over
2 cups sugar
1 cup water
1 long curl of lemon zest

Simmer cranberries, sugar, water, and lemon zest together until cranberries are split and falling apart, about 1 hour. Press the cranberry mixture through a chinoise or fine-mesh sieve to make a smooth purée. Freeze in an ice cream maker. Serve garnished with Concord grape halves and Basic Sweetened Cranberries (page 7).

Cape Cod October Pie

MAKES 8 SERVINGS

This pie has all the flavors of New England in the fall—and packs a wallop. It belies everything you've ever heard about the blandness of New England cooking.

Pastry for a two-crust pie
  (see following recipe)
1½ cups cranberries,
  coarsely chopped
1 cup peeled, cored, and diced
  apples
½ cup raisins

½ cup chopped walnuts
1½ cups sugar
2 tablespoons flour
1 teaspoon cinnamon
½ cup cranberry juice
1 teaspoon vanilla extract
4 tablespoons butter

Preheat oven to 425° F.

Line a 9-inch pie plate with pastry rolled to ⅛-inch thickness. Toss together the cranberries, apples, raisins, and walnuts with the sugar, flour, cinnamon, cranberry juice, and vanilla. Spoon lightly into unbaked pie shell and dot with butter. Cut strips from remaining pie crust and make a lattice over the top of the pie. Bake for about 40 minutes, until fruits are tender and pastry is brown.

Crust

2 cups sifted all-purpose flour | *⅓ cup shortening*
1 teaspoon salt | *⅓ cup ice water*

In a large mixing bowl, sift together the flour and salt. Cut or rub in the shortening very quickly, until the mixture resembles cornmeal. Add the ice water and toss the pastry together with a fork, stirring to the center until the pastry forms a ball. (Do not work the pastry; it will fall together.) Divide the pastry into two parts, form each into a ball, wrap in plastic, and chill at least 1 hour.

BLUEBERRIES

Intensely blue-purple with a deceptively mild flavor, blueberries are tiny (even in the large, cultivated version) and drolly beautiful. The blueberry flower leaves its stamen behind in a circular frill that decorates each fruit; properly fresh berries have a mauve blush overlying the deep blue, making them look frosted. The blueberry is one of three fruits native to America (the other two are the cranberry and the papaw), and of the three the most distinctive and certainly the most masculine. Blueberries have almost no acid content, so they are a perfect marriage with wine in desserts and sauces—I'm especially fond of them with Zinfandels and Cabernet Sauvignons.

Because of their mildness, it's almost impossible to use too much blueberry flavor—more is almost always better. And the flavor, when concentrated in a sauce, is satisfying in the same way a meat essence is satisfying—it is deep, basic, and unemphatic, its richness almost unobtrusive. And combining them with meat glazes and rich stocks creates pan sauces that are reverberatingly satisfying.

Native to the north, where summers are mild enough not to scorch the delicate fruit, blueberries have a sweet mythology, especially for New Englanders. My beau was raised on Cape Cod, and still knows the fields and empty lots that harbor blueberry bushes. Peter La Rivière, an American cook of some distinction, told me that his first and best memories of food were of following his gray-eyed Irish mama down to the back lot where the blueberries grew, carrying his own small pail for picking, and coming back with eight blueberries in the pail and about a quart inside him, his pinafore stained from neck to hem with that unmistakable color. It's still possible to pick blueberries wild in suburban and rural New England and in the mid-Atlantic, but the summer season sees thousands of pints of blues coming into supermarkets from Maine, which grows the tiny low-bush berries, and New Jersey and Pennsylvania, which produce the larger, even milder high-bush variety.

The built-in contrast of the blueberry—its intensity of color and its mildness of flavor—make it a perfect combination for the subtle but rich flavor of domestically raised game. Quail, buffalo, venison, partridge, and squab all taste wonderful stuffed and sauced with blueberries, which is no accident since most of these animals eagerly ate the fruit when they lived in the wild. It's important not to pair the blueberry with any flavor that will overwhelm its mildness, since it's possible to be left with the impression that it's all color and no taste. But used in large amounts and combined with other good flavors that aren't too emphatic, it's one of the most satisfying of all fruits.

I've given a number of recipes here that use blueberries more than one way in the same dish (like the quail) or concentrate the flavor by combining it with something very mild as a foil (like the slump). And don't forget, sometime during the season, to have a big bowl of fresh, just-washed blueberries with cream and a little sugar. And if you're in the right part of the country, be sure to find your local blueberry bush and stand in front of it in the early morning, or at dusk, and eat them straight from the twig, until your hands are dyed blue and the front of your shirt is as stained as Peter's pinafore was.

SOME BASICS

※

Frozen Blueberries

Like cranberries, blueberries can be frozen by scattering them on a cookie sheet and putting them in a sub-zero freezer, then bagging them for future use. Try to avoid commercially frozen berries that are partially cooked or frozen with water and sugar, unless you're planning to use them as purée or juice.

Sweetened Cooked Blueberries

MAKES 2½ CUPS

2 cups fresh blueberries,
    washed and picked over
    for stems

2 tablespoons water
⅔ cup sugar

Simmer all ingredients together just until the blueberries begin to soften, about 20 minutes.

Basic Blueberry Sauce

MAKES 2½ CUPS

2 cups fresh blueberries,
   washed and picked over
   for stems
2 tablespoons water

⅔ cup sugar
1 long curl of lemon zest
Juice of half a lemon
Pinch of ground cloves

Simmer all ingredients together until blueberries begin to dissolve, about 45 minutes. Use on ice cream, swirled into custard, or over cake. For purée, whiz briefly in food processor and strain through a chinoise or fine-mesh sieve.

SMALL PLATES

※

Cranberry Pemikan with Blueberry Sauce

MAKES 16 PATTIES

I've named this dish after a staple of American explorers, who probably adapted it from an Indian dish. Originally, the meats were dried, or jerked, and minced with dried fruits and nuts to carry on long trips into unknown territory where the food supply was uncertain. This is a settler's version, using fresh ingredients instead of dried, and combining two native American fruits in one dish—the sharpness of cranberry and the simplicity of blueberry. It's a fine beginner before a light main course, but is also good for breakfast, or better yet, brunch.

1 pound ground venison
¾ pound ground pork
3 teaspoons fresh-ground
    black pepper
1 teaspoon cayenne
2 teaspoons salt
1 teaspoon allspice
2 cups cranberries, washed
    and picked over
1 tablespoon chopped parsley
1 cup minced onion

2 teaspoons minced garlic
½ cup coarse-chopped black
    walnuts
½ cup dried juniper berries,
    soaked in 1 cup of boiling
    water for 30 minutes, then
    strained*
Basic Blueberry Sauce (see
    preceding recipe), made
    with ½ cup sugar

Work the venison and the pork together with clean hands until thoroughly blended, then blend in all other ingredients. Form into 2-ounce patties and cook on a hot grill or in a hot, dry cast-iron pan until brown on the outside and just past pink at the center, about 3 minutes to the side.

(continued)

As an appetizer, serve on small plates, the patties resting on a pool of blueberry sauce, garnished with scallion brushes and watercress.

For breakfast, serve with Corn Batter Cakes (page 34), and blueberry sauce.

* Juniper berries are available dried on most supermarket spice shelves.

Warm Scallops with Blueberry-Tarragon Dressing

SERVES 4

This is a light-as-a-feather first course that depends on the quiet flavors of scallop and blueberry and the spark of tarragon and orange for its considerable charm. Blueberries are as mild in flavor as they are intense in color and should almost always be paired with mildness to keep the tastes in balance.

1 pound sea scallops
4 cups white wine
2 cups water
2 bay leaves
2 celery ribs
4 large parsley sprigs
1 fresh tarragon branch
1 teaspoon red pepper flakes
1 teaspoon salt
1 teaspoon cracked
　peppercorns

1 lemon, quartered
½ orange, quartered
¼ cup light olive oil
½ cup orange juice
2 cups Blueberry-Tarragon
　Dressing (see following
　recipe)
For garnish: 4 unpeeled thin
　orange slices, 1 cup
　blueberries, and fresh
　tarragon leaves

Slice the scallops about ¼ inch thick. Boil together the wine, water, and all the seasonings; squeeze the lemon and orange into the mixture, then drop in the peels. Bring to a full rolling boil for 20 minutes, lower to a dimpled simmer (the liquid should just move at the surface, creating dimples), and slip the scallop slices into the pan. Cook for just 4 minutes and then remove scallops from liquid with a slotted spoon and put them, one layer deep, on a platter. Drizzle with olive oil and orange juice.

To serve, put a pool of dressing on each of four glass plates, then overlap the drained scallop slices in a circle on the dressing. Garnish with orange slices, blueberries, and fresh tarragon leaves.

Blueberry-Tarragon Dressing

¼ cup Sweetened Cooked
  Blueberries (page 25)
1 curl of orange zest

1 fresh tarragon branch
2 tablespoons red wine
1½ cups yogurt

Cook blueberries together with orange zest, tarragon, and red wine until they are very soft, about 30 minutes. Remove tarragon branch and orange zest and purée; strain. Beat the purée together with the yogurt and serve at once.

MAIN COURSES

※

Turkey Salad with Blueberries

SERVES 4

This low-fat, protein-rich salad is the perfect background for the subtle taste of blueberries. A drizzle of honey will sweeten it nicely, but the flavors are fresher with nothing added. Great for lunch with pumpernickel toast and iced tea. Or try it in smaller portions as a first course before something rich.

3 cups chicken stock
3 cups dry white wine
½ turkey breast, on the bone
2 pints blueberries, wild or
  cultivated
1½ cups jicama cut into
  1-inch julienne

2 cups low-fat yogurt
Salt and pepper to taste
2 small cantaloupes
8 large red-leaf lettuce leaves

Bring chicken stock and wine to a boil and lower to a simmer; add the turkey breast and cook for about 45 minutes, or until the meat is just beyond pink at the bone. Remove from liquid and cool briefly; bone breast and chill.

Pick over blueberries for stems and imperfect berries; drop jicama and blueberries into a bowl of ice water and refrigerate. Cut boned, chilled turkey breast into ½-inch cubes and toss with the yogurt, the well-drained jicama and all but 1 cup of the blueberries, salt, and pepper. Peel, halve, and seed the cantaloupes and slice each half into ¼-inch crescents. Arrange two lettuce leaves on each of four cold glass plates and fan half a cantaloupe's crescents on each. Pile a quarter of the turkey salad on each fan of cantaloupe and sprinkle with a few of the remaining blueberries.

Buffalo Steaks with Blueberry-Zinfandel Sauce

SERVES 4

This dish has some great flavors, but what makes it a killer are the colors. Buffalo is darker and richer in color than beef, and the blueberry purée is the perfect purple-blue background for that dark redness; the dark green of the watercress completes the picture.

4 buffalo sirloin strips, each about 8 ounces (about ½ inch thick)*
¾ cup balsamic vinegar
2 teaspoons Dijon mustard
1 teaspoon grated lemon peel
2 cups soy oil
2 cups wild blueberries, washed and picked over

¼ cup Zinfandel
¼ cup sugar
½ lemon, in two pieces
Pinch of ground allspice
Salt and pepper to taste

FOR GARNISH
1 cup blueberries and 4 large watercress sprigs

Trim all fat from steaks. Beat vinegar, mustard, and lemon peel together and add oil very slowly to emulsify; take care not to let oil and vinegar separate. Marinate steaks in vinaigrette 1 hour.

Meanwhile, simmer blueberries, wine, sugar, lemon, and allspice in a nonreactive pan until blueberries are falling apart, about 30 minutes. Force mixture through a chinoise or fine-mesh sieve and season the resulting purée with salt and pepper.

Grill the steaks on a medium-hot charcoal fire, 4 minutes to the side, or sear them in a hot cast-iron skillet and finish in a hot oven, for about 20 minutes. They should be medium rare. Let the steaks rest in a warm place.

Heat the blueberry purée until just hot, and divide it among four hot dinner plates. Slice each steak medium-thick and fan in a semicircle on each plate. Garnish with the watercress and blueberries.

Wonderful as an accompaniment and beautiful on the plate: baked, peeled, sliced sweet potatoes.

* Buffalo can be found in specialty butcher shops.

Three-Blueberry Quail with Corn Batter Cakes

SERVES 4

One of the pleasures of blueberries is that their suave, subtle taste lets you use them in layers and quantities—there's no need to think in terms of a *hint* of blueberry. The more, the better. Here blueberries are used to stuff the quail, to sauce it, and, in batter cakes, to bed it. It's the multiplication of blueberry that lets the flavor come through. Some flavors have a natural affinity: Blueberries go very well with the rich flavors of game, and the sweetness of cornmeal is always great with them.

12 quail*
1½ pounds ground pork
1 teaspoon allspice
2 teaspoons fresh-ground
    black pepper
1½ teaspoons salt
½ teaspoon cayenne
2 teaspoons chopped fresh
    thyme, or 1 teaspoon dried
1 tablespoon fine-chopped
    fresh parsley
1½ pints wild blueberries,
    washed and picked over
6 slices bacon, ¼ inch thick,
    cut in half

2 cups chicken stock
1 cup white wine
¼ pound butter
1 bay leaf
1 teaspoon chopped fresh
    thyme
2 teaspoons brown sugar
1 pint wild blueberries,
    washed and picked over
8 Corn Batter Cakes (see
    following recipe)

FOR GARNISH
baby chicory

Preheat oven to 425° F.

Wash and dry quail; trim necks close to bodies. Mix ground pork with spices, herbs, and salt and pepper; work blueberries into sausage mixture. Stuff quails with the sausage. Arrange on a rack in a roaster pan, making sure to leave plenty of room between birds. Lay a half-slice of bacon across the breast of each bird. Roast for 30 to 40 minutes, or until the breast is brown and the meat is still just pink at the bone. During the last 15 minutes of cooking, baste twice with warm chicken stock, wine, and butter melted together. When they're done, remove birds from the pan and stir the juices from the bottom. If necessary, add chicken stock and wine to make 3 cups. Add bay leaf, thyme, and brown sugar and reduce at a gentle simmer to 2 cups. Strain, add 2 cups blueberries, and simmer just until they begin to pop. For each serving, set 3 quail in a tight circle, legs facing inward, on two overlapping corn batter cakes and pour sauce over the quail. Garnish with baby chicory leaves.

* Quail are now domestically raised all over the country; the ones we get in the Northeast are from North Carolina. Check with your butcher to see if he carries them, or, if not, if he can order them.

Corn Batter Cakes

MAKES 18 TO 20 CAKES

2½ cups milk
2½ cups water
1½ cups cornmeal
3 cups all-purpose flour
3 teaspoons baking powder
1 teaspoon baking soda

1 teaspoon salt
4 eggs
½ pound butter, melted
2 cups wild blueberries,
    washed and picked over

In a 3-quart saucepan, heat the milk and water together to scalding; sprinkle the cornmeal on the surface of the milk mixture and whisk it in, sprinkling and whisking constantly until the cornmeal is entirely absorbed. Whip until the mixture is smooth and the cornmeal is cooked, about 3 minutes. Cool to room temperature.

Sift together flour, baking powder, soda, and salt. Beat eggs and melted butter together. Stir dry ingredients and egg mixture into the cornmeal mixture in alternate spoonfuls, beating constantly with a wire whisk. Let stand for 10 minutes. Just before cooking, fold in the blueberries.

Cook on a lightly greased hot griddle, allowing about ¼ cup batter per cake. Be sure to let each cake set well before turning; they are very delicate and will tear easily.

DESSERTS

Blueberry Biscuit Cobbler

SERVES 6

New England produces more small, low-bush blueberries than any other region, and has an extraordinary number of recipes for them; this cross between shortcake and cobbler takes advantage of the smooth texture of both blueberries and the dough topping.

4 cups all-purpose flour
¼ cup baking powder
1½ teaspoons salt
⅔ cup sugar
1 cup shortening
3 cups milk

6 cups low-bush blueberries
Juice and grated zest of 1 lemon
½ teaspoon ground cloves
1½ cups sugar
¼ cup flour

Preheat oven to 400° F.

Sift together flour, baking powder, salt, and sugar. Work in shortening with a pastry blender or your clean hands, until mixture is the texture of oatmeal. Add the milk, stirring just long enough for the dry mixture to absorb the liquid. The dough should be very soft.

Stem and wash the blueberries and toss with the lemon zest and juice. Sift together the cloves, sugar, and flour and layer with the blueberries in a 2-quart roasting pan.

Pat the dough out on a floured surface to a thickness of about ½ inch and cut into 3-inch rounds. Top the blueberries with the rounds, letting them almost touch at the edges. Bake for about 1 hour, until the biscuits have risen and are golden brown and the blueberries are thick and bubbly.

Serve at once in deep bowls with heavy cream.

Red, White, and Blueberry Shortcake

SERVES 8

This is our Fourth of July dessert at Miss Ruby's Cafe. It is festive, colorful, and as American as the Stars and Stripes.

2 cups strawberries, hulled
  and washed
1½ cups sugar
3 cups blueberries, washed
  and picked over
Juice of ½ lemon
2 cups all-purpose flour,
  sifted

½ teaspoon salt
2½ teaspoons baking powder
¾ cup vegetable shortening
3 cups milk
1 cup whipping cream
¼ cup confectioners' sugar

Slice strawberries, reserving 8 for garnish, and toss with ½ cup sugar. Refrigerate. Toss blueberries (reserve ½ cup for garnish) with ½ cup sugar and lemon juice and warm very slightly in a nonreactive saucepan. When sugar has melted, mash slightly and refrigerate.

Preheat oven to 425° F.

Sift together flour, salt, 7 tablespoons sugar, and baking powder. Cut in vegetable shortening until mixture is the consistency of oatmeal. Stir in milk, mixing just until all the dry mixture is absorbed.

Turn onto floured board and roll to ½-inch thickness. Cut an 8-inch round and, using a spatula, lift onto an ungreased cookie sheet. Brush with milk and sprinkle with remaining tablespoon sugar. Bake 12 to 15 minutes, or until golden brown and fully risen.

While the biscuit is baking, whip the cream, adding the confectioners' sugar when it is almost fully thickened.

When biscuit is done, remove from oven, split and spread with butter. Put the bottom half on a 12-inch dessert plate and pile one side with strawberries, letting them spill onto the plate. Pile the other side with the blueberries and put a stripe of whipped cream in the middle. Cover with the top half of the biscuit and add more whipped cream. Decorate with whole strawberries and a sprinkle of blueberries. Serve at once.

Blueberry-Nectarine Pie with Cornflour Pastry

SERVES 8

This is a version of the pie that my agent, a Yale lawyer with a mind like a steel trap and a voice like a silver bell, uses to woo anyone of her acquaintaince not already lulled into a state of happy acquiescence.

3 cups sliced nectarines	Pinch of ground cloves
1½ cups sugar	Cornflour Pastry for a
½ teaspoon almond extract	double-crust pie (see
Juice and grated zest of 1	following recipe)
lemon	1 tablespoon flour
1½ cups large blueberries,	2 tablespoons butter
washed and picked over	

Preheat oven to 375° F.

Toss nectarines with 1 cup of sugar, almond extract, and lemon juice and zest; toss blueberries with ½ cup sugar and pinch of cloves. Roll out half the pie crust and line an 8-inch pie shell. Sprinkle flour on the pastry. Pile nectarines into the pie shell, then scatter blueberries on the surface of the nectarines. Dot the fruit with the butter. Roll out the top pastry and cut into fanciful shapes with a cookie cutter. Arrange on top of the fruit so that it's covered about as densely as it would be by a lattice crust. Bake for 45 minutes, or until crust is golden brown.

Cornflour Pastry

PASTRY FOR A DOUBLE-CRUST PIE

2 cups all-purpose flour
1 cup masa (Spanish
  cornflour)
1 teaspoon baking powder

1 teaspoon salt
1½ cups vegetable shortening
4 tablespoons ice water

Sift together flour, cornflour, baking powder, and salt. Cut in short-ening until mixture resembles fine oatmeal. Add water, tossing quickly just until water is absorbed and pastry will roll together in a ball. Chill for 30 minutes to 1 hour.

Adirondack Chocolate Ice Cream

SERVES 12

This is from the cookbook of a dedicated Greenwich Village cook, John Bergamini, who was born and raised in Lake Placid and whose family passed on a lot of cooking lore, including the legend that this dessert was invented by the Whitneys' cook at their Adirondack compound. It's a wonderful and totally unexpected combination, no matter how high or low its provenance.

6 ounces unsweetened chocolate	½ teaspoon salt
2 quarts half and half	1 teaspoon vanilla
2 cups sugar	2 cups maple syrup
24 egg yolks	2 cups wild blueberries, picked over and washed

Melt chocolate over hot water. Scald half and half. Beat egg yolks with sugar and salt. Add a cup of the hot half and half to the egg yolk mixture, then beat that mixture into the rest of the hot half and half and cook over a very low flame until mixture thickens enough to coat a spoon. Add vanilla; beat in melted chocolate. Freeze in rotary freezer, hand powered or electric. When the ice cream is frozen, pack in quart containers and freeze hard in freezing compartment of refrigerator. Serve with maple syrup and blueberries.

OTHER GOOD THINGS

⬙

Some of the best uses of the very basic flavor of blueberries are so simple that they are hardly recipes at all, just instructions. Here are a few of them:

BLUEBERRY MUFFINS: Substitute 1¼ cups wild blueberries tossed with a teaspoon of lemon juice for the cranberries in the Cranberry Muffin recipe (page 17).

BLUEBERRY PIE: Use 4 cups of blueberries and 1 cup of blueberry purée (see Basic Blueberry Sauce, page 26) in place of the blueberries and nectarines in the Blueberry and Nectarine Pie (page 36). Omit the almond extract.

BLUEBERRY SWIRL ICE CREAM Make the Corn Ice Cream (page 72), omitting both kinds of corn; stir in 2 cups of blueberry purée (see Basic Blueberry Sauce, page 26), with 1 extra cup of sugar. Freeze hard in your freezer.

BLUEBERRY FRUIT PLATE Blueberries make a great combination with other mild, classic fruits and cheeses. Serve a plate of pears, blueberries, cantaloupe slices, and bananas, paired with mascarpone, brie, and Double Gloucester.

BLUEBERRY TOPPING Thin the Sweetened Cooked Blueberries (page 25) slightly with grape juice, and use on ice cream, waffles, or pancakes, especially the Corn Batter Cakes in the quail recipe (page 34).

BLACKBERRIES

T his is the fruit we all waited for every summer—though in Texas blackberry season was early summer, not late. But as soon as school was out, we were looking forward to that moment when every ditch in the county would be filled with brambles—which scratched the hands—loaded with long, many-globed berries—which stained the hands. I don't remember getting any blackberries into the house; all my memories are of eating them off the brambles, as my grandmother ate figs off her trees in the summer mornings, "to save them from the birds." But there must have been someone picking and bringing home, because I know we had blackberry pies and cobblers and tarts, and that every now and again someone would make syrup. It is still, for me, the most intense and evocative fruit flavor—I regret only that there is no blackberry *eau de vie* to give me that flavor without a hint of acidity or sweetness.

I can't direct you to the blackberry brambles of the Texas countryside, but if you have brambles of your own, I urge you to eat as many as you can straight from the vine. Once you're home and in the kitchen, and the fruit sits tamed in a bucket, ready to be turned into something more than pure blackberry—even by the mere addition of sugar and cream—you've lost that moment when you're part of mornings when the world was young and there was no reason not to eat what you found. Don't lose it, even if you don't get home with enough berries to make *anything!*

Every one of us who had a berry-picking childhood knows the magic of finding the fruit on the bramble—suddenly every summer, as if there had never been a berry before. Some of us, now city dwellers, may never have those moments again, but we stay ready for them in some way, as if the park, or a highway esplanade, or a random pitch of grass will suddenly sprout a bush with those precious jewel-colored fruits hiding among the tangle. We carry with us the odor of warm berries in pails and the memories of stains on T-shirts and scratches on hands and arms. And if we are in the country, and the berries are there again, in a ditch, in the back of an empty lot, in someone's backyard, it's as if the taste of the berries themselves, as luscious as it is, is not as powerful as the memories returning with the reality of picking them.

SOME BASICS

Blackberries, like raspberries, are multiple fruits—that is, each berry is really a dozen or more tiny fruits in a cluster, each with its own seed. Each tiny fruit is called a drupelet, and I defy you to say that twice without breaking up. Go ahead. The drupelets aren't the problem, however; it's the seeds. All those seeds make the cooking of blackberries a vexing business, since the flesh of the fruit tends to collapse, leaving you uncomfortably aware of seeds. This happens, too, if the blackberries aren't quite fresh and the flesh has begun to dry around the seeds. So I've provided some solutions: to get rid of the seeds entirely, or to avoid cooking, so that the problem of the seeds is negligible.

So it pays to buy or pick the fruit absolutely fresh, and to cook it lightly if at all, or to use it in some seedless form: To that end, there are a few basic preparations that make the whole process much easier.

Blackberry Purée

MAKES 4½ CUPS

1 quart perfectly fresh
  blackberries, washed and
  picked over

1½ cups sugar

Put blackberries in the bowl of a food processor along with the sugar. Process, pulsing, until blackberries are reduced to a fine pulp. Do not overprocess, or purée will become juice and seeds will be pulverized, ruining the fruit's taste. Press through a sieve just fine enough to contain the seeds. Sugar may be omitted.

Blackberry Juice

MAKES 4½ CUPS

1 quart perfectly fresh
   blackberries, washed and
   picked over
1 cup water

1½ cups sugar

Simmer blackberries with water until they are dissolved, about 40 minutes. Add sugar and cook further until the mixture is a thick liquid. Strain through a chinoise or fine-mesh sieve. Sugar may be omitted.

Blackberry Jam

MAKES 6 CUPS

1 quart perfectly fresh
   blackberries, washed and
   picked over
1½ cups plus ½ cup sugar

1 cup unpeeled apple slices
1 cup water
1 pint Blackberry Purée
   (page 43)

Toss blackberries with 1½ cups sugar and let stand. Cook apples in the water until they are reduced to a mush. Strain through the finest sieve. Reheat with ½ cup sugar. Add blackberry purée and stir. Add blackberries and simmer for about 20 minutes, or until apples and blackberries are well combined. Chill or jar, using the boiling-water-bath canning method.

SMALL PLATES

✖

Blackberries and Watercress

SERVES 4

2 bunches watercress
1 pint blackberries, washed
    and picked over
1 tablespoon Dijon mustard

⅓ cup blackberry vinegar
1 teaspoon salt
1 teaspoon pepper
1 cup light olive oil

Wash watercress and spin dry. Put blackberries in a large colander and spray them lightly with water. Turn out on a towel to dry.

Beat mustard, vinegar, salt, and pepper together, then add oil slowly until the dressing is emulsified. Toss watercress with ⅓ cup dressing and top with blackberries. Serve at once.

Berry Chicken Salad

SERVES 4

1 head salad bowl lettuce,
  washed, dried, and
  separated
16 chicken tenderloins,
  poached
2 celery ribs from the heart,
  cut on the diagonal into
  2-inch pieces

1 tablespoon Dijon mustard
⅓ cup blackberry vinegar
1 teaspoon salt
1 teaspoon pepper
1 cup light olive oil
1 pint blackberries, washed
  and picked over

Arrange lettuce leaves on a glass platter and toss chicken and celery together with ⅓ cup of the dressing. Arrange on the lettuce. Strew with blackberries.

MAIN COURSES

※

Blackberry Pork Chops with Apple Stuffing

SERVES 4

I love these because they combine two of the favorite flavors of my childhood—the rich, satisfying taste of smothered pork and the fresh summer goodness of blackberries. It's half surprising, and entirely a pleasure.

4 loin pork chops, about 2
   inches thick
1 cup thin-sliced apples
¼ cup sugar tossed with ½
   teaspoon each salt and
   pepper
½ teaspoon cinnamon
2 cups all-purpose flour
1 teaspoon salt
1 teaspoon pepper

4 tablespoons butter
3 cups chicken stock
½ cup sweetened Blackberry
   Purée (page 43)
½ cup unsweetened
   Blackberry Purée
1 pint perfectly fresh
   blackberries, washed and
   picked over

Cut a slit in each pork chop from the side; toss apple slices with sugar and cinnamon and stuff each chop with apples. If necessary, fasten slit with a toothpick. Dredge pork chops in flour, salt, and pepper. Melt butter in a heavy skillet with a top; when foam subsides, brown chops on both sides. Add chicken stock, cover skillet, and turn heat down. Simmer until chops are done through, and tender, about 1 hour. Remove chops from stock and set in a warm place; skim off all fat. Boil down stock to half its volume and add purées; stir to combine.

Pour sauce onto an oval platter and arrange chops on top. Strew with blackberries.

Venison Shoulder with Dried-Fruit Dressing

SERVES 12

THE MARINADE
1 cup balsamic vinegar
½ cup olive oil
2 oranges, sliced
1 lemon, sliced
2 garlic cloves, chopped
4 whole cloves
1 whole allspice berry, cracked
1 bay leaf

4 crushed juniper berries
1 large yellow onion, sliced
2 celery ribs, with leaves, sliced
½ fennel bulb, sliced

1 shoulder roast of venison, about
  4 pounds, boned and
  butterflied, with bones reserved

THE STOCK
1 large yellow onion, chopped
2 celery ribs, with leaves,
  sliced
1 large carrot, sliced
4 cups dry red wine
8 cracked black peppercorns

8 cracked green peppercorns
½ bunch parsley
2 sage branches
4 thyme branches
2 bay leaves
6 juniper berries, bruised

THE STUFFING
2 cups dried apples
1 cup dried pitted prunes
½ cup brown sugar
½ cup blackberry brandy
½ cup unsweetened
  Blackberry Purée (page 43)
½ cup cognac
1 medium yellow onion

1 celery rib
¼ pound butter
1 teaspoon salt
1 teaspoon pepper
2 teaspoons chopped sage leaves
3 teaspoons chopped fresh thyme
2 cups French bread cubes

4 thick slices double-smoked
  bacon
¼ pound butter and 2 cups
  red wine, simmered together
¼ cup flour
Juice of 1 orange and curl of
  zest of ½ orange

½ cup unsweetened
  blackberry juice
½ cup blackberry brandy
2 cups fresh whole blackberries

One day ahead, boil the marinade ingredients together. Pour over venison shoulder and set in refrigerator overnight, turning once.

Preheat oven to 400° F and brown in a roasting pan the reserved venison bones, onion, celery, and carrot with a drizzle of olive oil; this should take about 1½ hours. Deglaze the pan with the red wine and 4 cups of water. Simmer bones and vegetables in the wine and water, with more water to cover, along with the peppercorns, parsley, sage, thyme, bay leaves, and juniper berries, for about 6 hours, replenishing water as necessary. Do not boil. Strain stock and chill overnight.

For the stuffing, chop apples and prunes together and pour over them brown sugar, blackberry brandy, blackberry purée, and cognac. Toss together and refrigerate overnight.

On the day, skim stock and return to heat to reduce by half.

For the stuffing, dice medium onion and celery and sauté in butter with salt, pepper, sage, and thyme. Add bread cubes and toss together, adding more butter if the mixture is too dry. Add the apple and prune mixture and toss thoroughly to mix. Add 1 cup of the reduced stock.

Preheat oven to 425° F.

Remove venison from its marinade and dry with a damp towel. Spread the stuffing over the inside surface of the meat—do not be too generous; if stuffing is left over, put it in a small buttered pan and drizzle with a bit of the butter-red wine mixture. Roll and tie shoulder and place on a rack in a roasting pan; drape with the bacon slices. Roast about 1¼ hours, or until done but still pink at the center, basting every 20 minutes or so with red wine and butter.

When roast is done, remove from pan and let rest in a warm place. Remove rack and place pan over a medium flame. Sprinkle pan with flour and use a spatula to scrape the bottom, mixing flour with fat and other bits from the pan. Stir and scrape until flour is brown, about 5 minutes. Deglaze pan with reduced stock, scraping any residue from the bottom, and stir over a low flame until the sauce thickens slightly, about 10 minutes. Give the bottom of the pan a last scrape, paying careful attention to corners, and then strain into a saucepan. Bring to a simmer and add orange juice and zest, blackberry juice, and blackberry brandy; simmer 10 minutes.

Slice roast and serve with any extra stuffing under each slice, a spoonful of sauce on top, and a sprinkle of the fresh blackberries for garnish.

DESSERTS

※

Apple-Blackberry Pie

SERVES 8

I'm never very happy with cooked versions of the composite fruits; the tiny seeds that are part of the lusciousness of the uncooked fruit are a nuisance when the pulp is reduced by cooking. This pie solves the problems two ways: It uses blackberry juice to spread the flavor throughout the pie, and precooks the apples and the crust to keep the blackberries almost uncooked.

Butter Pastry for a double-crust pie (page 53)
4 cups peeled, sliced apples, greenings or Granny Smiths
2 cups sweetened blackberry juice

2 cups sugar
1 teaspoon allspice
2 cups fresh blackberries
¼ cup soft butter

Preheat oven to 400° F.

Make pastry and divide into two balls of equal size; chill briefly. Roll out one pastry ball and line an 8-inch pie pan with it. Line the pastry with foil and weight with rice or beans or another pie plate. Roll out second ball of dough and use cookie cutters to cut out 8 or 10 decorative pieces for the top. Place on a cookie sheet. Bake bottom crust and decorative pieces for 10 to 12 minutes, until just light golden brown. Remove weight from bottom crust.

Meanwhile, in a nonreactive saucepan, simmer apples with blackberry juice, stirring. When apples are just past crisp toward soft, add sugar tossed with the cinnamon and cook until sugar is melted and apples are soft but not mushy. Add blackberries and soft butter and toss together very gently. Pour mixture into warm pastry shell and decorate top with pastry shapes. Serve at once.

Blackberry Sorbet
with Raspberry Purée

SERVES 8

3 cups sweetened Blackberry
   Purée (page 43)
1 cup extra-fine sugar

½ cup crème de cassis
2 cups fresh raspberries
½ cup sugar

Stir blackberry purée, extra-fine sugar, and crème de cassis together and let stand about half an hour, until the sugar is melted. Freeze in a rotary freezer until firm, then transfer to a quart container and freeze hard in the freezer of the refrigerator.

Purée raspberries and sugar in the food processor and pass through a chinoise or fine-mesh sieve. Chill.

Serve scoops of sorbet on chilled glass plates, resting on small pools of raspberry purée.

Cassis-Blackberry Tart with Ginger Syrup

SERVES 8

1 recipe Butter Pastry (see
  following recipe)
3 cups half-and-half
4 whole eggs
2 egg yolks
1¾ cups sugar

¼ cup flour
¼ cup cassis
2 cups whole fresh
  blackberries
¼ cup water
1 ounce fresh ginger, chopped

Preheat oven to 400° F.

Roll out pastry and line an 8-inch fluted, straight-sided French tart pan with it. Weight the pastry with foil and beans or rice, or another, smaller pan, and bake for 12 or 13 minutes, until golden brown. Let cool.

Scald half-and-half; beat eggs and yolks together until light and fluffy; beat in ¾ cup of the sugar. Beat in ½ cup of the scalded half-and-half, then beat the egg mixture into the rest of the half-and-half over a very low flame. Beat just until the mixture begins to thicken; remove from flame and continue to beat, sifting in the flour. Add the cassis. When mixture is room temperature, spread the tart shell with the custard. Arrange the blackberries in a single layer on top of the pastry cream.

Melt remaining 1 cup sugar with the water and the chopped ginger and boil together for about 5 minutes. Strain and cool, then drizzle over the blackberries, being careful not to miss a berry. Serve at once or slightly chilled.

Butter Pastry

MAKES ONE 10-INCH
DOUBLE-CRUST PIE CRUST

2 cups sifted all-purpose flour
½ teaspoon salt
¾ cup (1½ sticks) very cold
unsalted butter

Ice water to mix (about 2
tablespoons)

Sift the flour and salt into a bowl. With two knives, a pastry cutter, or your fingers, very quickly and lightly cut the butter into flour. When the mixture is the texture of dry oatmeal, stir in the ice water with a fork. Blend just until the dry mixture absorbs the water and lightly holds together. If there are crumbs left around the ball of dough, add a smidgen more ice water. Without any further handling, wrap the dough in a square of plastic wrap and chill for 1 hour or more. Divide the dough into two equal parts, and quickly and firmly roll out on a floured board to a thickness of ⅛ inch.

CORN

❖

Of all the ingredients I write about, corn is the one that best illustrates this book's thesis: American cooking is a treasure-house of food, hardly recognized outside its borders, and rarely recognized professionally at home. Corn is extraordinary in flavor, colorful, full of food value, and usable in a multitude of forms. Dried corn, in the varieties Europeans feed to animals, is used for hominy, grits, cornmeal (which becomes corn bread, cornmeal mush, spoonbread, batter cakes, and tortillas); fresh corn on the cob (and cut off) in the sweet varieties we've developed in the last fifty years, is Lucullan: It is best, like asparagus, in its youngest and simplest forms. Its season is short, its flavor unparalleled, and it is best to get as much as possible of it while you can, in late July, August, and September. Corn is in our diets, too, in ways we hardly notice: These days corn syrup is more often used for sweetening prepared foods than sugar, cornstarch is ubiquitous as a thickener, and corn continues to be the basis of the greatest of the native American whiskies.

Of course, even in its less luscious forms, frozen and canned, corn can serve as the basis of great dishes: Good corn pudding, for instance, is perfectly possible made with the canned or frozen kernels, and combining cornmeal with frozen or canned corn can enrich both. In general, Americans feel about corn the way they do about tomatoes: Fresh is best, but if that's not available, the shortest distance to some form of the vegetable is worth taking.

Corn is also ubiquitously American: It's possible to think of cornmeal preparations as more typical of the South, but the Midwest grows and eats corn in abundance, the Northeast first took it from the Indians and made it its own with Indian pudding and Johnny-cake, and in the Southwest it usually has a Spanish accent, as tortillas or posole; lately in California, tiny ears of the youngest fresh corn are eaten raw and whole, husks and all, as salads. No matter where you are in this country, there will be some kind of corn dish, sure to be typical of the region.

SMALL PLATES

Corn and Red Onion Fritters with Pimiento-Jalapeño Sauce

MAKES 2 DOZEN FRITTERS

This is Charlie Kahlstrom's fritter recipe, the one he saved the restaurant with: We were making fritters that sank with a dull thud and seemed to survive in the memory for days. Charlie worked until he had this light and satisfying recipe, which is on our menu all the time; the basic batter is infinitely variable with other ingredients—cinnamon and apple, fennel, clam and oregano, and on and on—but it's the classic corn recipe that I'm always being asked for.

2 cups all-purpose flour
1 cup pastry flour
2 tablespoons baking powder
1 teaspoon salt
2 eggs
2 cups diced red onions
3 cups corn kernels and their milk, fresh off the ear, or 3 cups canned corn with its juice

Milk to moisten, about 1½ cups
1½ quarts soy oil

Sift together flours, baking powder, and salt. Stir in all other ingredients but milk, then moisten with just enough milk to produce a dropping batter, about 1½ cups.

Heat oil to 375° F, and drop in fritters by the generous teaspoonful. Fry until golden brown, about 5 minutes.

The Sauce

MAKES 8 CUPS

This sauce is really a version of my mother's chile con queso, usually served in Texas with tortilla chips. It is also good poured over hot open-face chicken sandwiches, steamed broccoli, or baked tomatoes. Given some thought, it can be tried on anything that occurs to you —unless you're put off by the heat of the jalepeños.

¼ pound unsalted butter
¾ cup flour
6 cups milk
¼ pound sharp Cheddar
  cheese, grated

1½ cups chopped jalapeños
  en escabeche (pickled) and
  their juice
2 cups chopped pimientos and
  their juice

In a 2-quart saucepan, melt butter and stir in flour; cook, stirring, for 10 minutes without browning. Meanwhile, scald the milk; add milk to roux all at once, whisking constantly. Whisk until smooth, then add cheese and stir until melted and sauce is smooth. Stir in peppers and pimientos. Add salt as necessary.

Black Bean
Corn Batter Cakes with
Citrus Salsa and Sour Cream

MAKES 25 TO 30 CAKES, OR 10 SERVINGS

This recipe is based on a whole category of great dishes that originated in Virginia—dishes begun by scalding cornmeal with milk or water, cooling the resulting mush, and then beating eggs into it. Spoonbread, batter cakes, and hot-water corn bread are all made this way. When the mixture is baked or cooked on a griddle, the cooked cornmeal expands and creates a soufflé-like texture that is as light as it is satisfying. This use of the batter cake, giving a southwestern accent to a classic southern dish, is one of Cathy Casey's inspirations, an improvisatory special she created at Miss Ruby's one night when batter cakes were on the menu.

2½ cups milk	½ pound butter, melted
2½ cups water	2 cups cooked black beans, rinsed
1½ cups cornmeal	
3 cups all-purpose flour	2 cups sour cream
3 teaspoons baking powder	Citrus Salsa (see following recipe)
1 teaspoon salt	
1 tablespoon ground cumin	Sprigs of fresh coriander for garnish
4 eggs	

In a 3-quart saucepan over a medium flame, heat the milk and water together to scalding; sprinkle the cornmeal on the surface of the milk mixture and whisk it in, sprinkling and whisking constantly until the cornmeal is entirely absorbed. Whip until the mixture is smooth and the cornmeal is cooked, about 3 minutes. Cool to room temperature.

Sift together flour, baking powder, salt, and cumin. Beat eggs and melted butter together. Stir dry ingredients and egg mixture into the

(continued)

cornmeal mixture in alternate spoonfuls, beating constantly with a wire whisk. Let stand for 10 minutes. Just before cooking, stir in the black beans.

Cook on a lightly greased hot griddle, allowing about 2 tablespoons of batter to the cake. Be sure to let each cake set well before turning; they are very delicate and will tear easily.

Overlap three small batter cakes in a circle on an 8-inch plate. Top with a generous tablespoon of salsa and a dollop of sour cream. Decorate with a sprig of coriander.

Citrus Salsa

MAKES 2 CUPS

Supremes (skinned sections)
and grated zest of 1 large
orange
Supremes and grated zest of 1
pink grapefruit
2 large fresh tomatoes, peeled
and diced fine
4 scallions, green and white
parts, sliced very thin

2 tablespoons chopped fresh
coriander
1 tablespoon canned chipotle,
chopped fine
Salt, black pepper, and
Tabasco to taste

Chop the supremes into small pieces. Toss tomatoes, scallions, orange and zest, grapefruit and zest, and coriander together. Season to taste and serve at once.

Confetti Creamed Corn and Wild Boar Sausage on Cheddar Pastries

SERVES 6 TO 8

THE SAUSAGE
1 pound wild boar shoulder,
    ground*
1 pound ground pork
1 tablespoon ground allspice
1 tablespoon ground black
    pepper
2 teaspoons cayenne

3 tablespoons chopped fresh
    thyme
12 poached, bruised juniper
    berries
1 tablespoon salt
4 tablespoons chopped fresh
    parsley

THE PASTRY
2 cups flour
1 teaspoon salt
5 tablespoons cold butter

¼ pound sharp Cheddar
    cheese, grated
Cold water

THE CORN
6 thick slices bacon, diced
4 tablespoons butter
1 cup diced green peppers
1 cup diced red peppers
⅔ cup diced celery
½ cup diced red onion
4 tablespoons flour

4 cups corn kernels, cut off
    the cob (a robust yellow
    variety like golden Bantam
    is good for this dish)
Salt and pepper to taste
6 cups milk

Combine all the sausage ingredients, mashing together with your clean hands. Form into patties of about 3 ounces each, making about 10.

Grill sausages over charcoal, about three inches from medium-hot coals, 4 minutes to the side; or cook in a dry, hot cast-iron skillet over a medium flame, 5 minutes to the side.

Preheat the oven to 400° F.

For the pastry, sift flour and salt together and work butter in with two knives or a pastry blender. Toss with Cheddar cheese, then add just enough cold water (about ¼ cup) to hold dough together. Form dough into a ball and chill for at least 1 hour. Roll dough to ⅛-inch thickness and cut into 4-inch rounds. Lay the rounds loosely on upended cupcake tins (they should form shallow baskets) and bake for 7 to 10 minutes, until light brown.

For the corn, fry bacon in a heavy 12-inch skillet over a medium flame until crisp. Remove bacon bits and reserve. Add butter to bacon fat and melt until it froths. Add peppers, celery, and onions and sauté until soft. Sprinkle flour, salt, and pepper on the vegetables and stir briskly until the flour is absorbed. Cook, stirring constantly, for about 5 minutes, or until flour is light tan. Add corn and its liquid and stir everything together. Add milk and stir until the mixture bubbles and thickens slightly.

Pour corn mixture into pastry cups and sprinkle reserved bacon pieces over the tops. Serve on small bright-colored plates with two sausage patties on the side.

* Boar is available at most specialty butchers; in New York, Ottomanelli's, and by mail from Noel Perrin at the Texas Wild Game Cooperative. P.O. Box 530, Ingram, TX 78025.

SOUPS

Corn and Lobster Chowder

SERVES 8

Chowders are classically American, usually thought of as a way to subsume a lot of not very classy seafood under a blanket of rich pork/milk/butter flavors. But when a chowder is made with young corn and lobster, those delicacies of the country, it becomes something to accompany with champagne and follow with fresh peaches. Try it that way.

2 ounces salt pork, cut into
   small cubes
4 tablespoons butter
1 large white onion, minced
2 large stalks celery, minced
2 tablespoons flour
1 lobster, about 2 pounds
1 teaspoon salt
1 bay leaf

2 thyme branches
3 cups corn kernels and their
   liquid, cut off the cob
   (about 8 ears)
4 cups half-and-half
Dash of Tabasco
½ teaspoon cayenne
Paprika

Render salt pork in a heavy 1-gallon Dutch oven. Meanwhile, bring 1 gallon water to a boil. Remove and reserve the salt pork cubes when golden brown, and melt the butter in the rendered pork fat. Add the minced onion and celery and sauté until transparent and soft. Sprinkle with flour, stir thoroughly to blend, and cook very slowly until the flour is thoroughly cooked but not browned, about 5 minutes.

When the water boils, kill the lobster by piercing behind the head, then plunge the lobster head first into the water; boil for 5 minutes, remove, and plunge into iced water. Split the lobster down the center of the tail and crack the claws. Using a cocktail fork or a small meat fork, pull the lobster meat from the claws and tail, and remove the coral and tomalley from the body (both are found in the center of the split body, between the tail and the head; the coral, which is present only if the lobster is female, is the lobster roe and is called after its color; the tomalley is the liver, and is green). In a saucepan, simmer the lobster shell in a quart of the water in which you boiled the lobster.

Add salt, bay leaf, and thyme to the flour-onion mixture, and stir for 2 minutes. Add the water strained from the lobster shell. Stir until the mixture is smooth. Simmer for 20 minutes. Add corn and half-and-half, Tabasco and cayenne, and simmer for another 15 minutes.

Cut the lobster meat into 1-inch chunks. When the soup is ready to serve, add the lobster meat and bring the soup to a simmer again. Serve with a sprinkle of paprika.

Corn Velvet with Red-Pepper Purée

SERVES 8

This is essence of corn, topped with the bright contrasting spritz of sweet red pepper.

8 cups heavy cream
4 cups (about 16 ears) of
  corn cut off the cob, with
  its liquid (reserve 6
  corncobs)

Salt and white pepper to taste
3 large red bell peppers

Pour the cream over the corncobs and bring to a boil; turn down the heat and simmer for about 45 minutes. Let the mixture cool slightly, then remove the corncobs. Add the corn kernels and their liquid to the cream. Simmer for another 30 minutes and then purée in the food processor until liquid. Strain through a chinoise or fine-mesh sieve, pressing to get all of the corn essence. Season with salt and pepper. Reheat to serve.

While the soup is simmering, roast the red peppers directly on the burner of the gas stove, turned high. Let them blacken, turning on all sides with a long fork or pair of tongs. Drop the blackened peppers into a paper bag and fasten closely. Let stand for 10 minutes, then remove from bag and peel. Purée the red flesh with 1 table-spoon water; add salt and pepper to taste.

Serve the soup with a swirl of the pepper purée on the surface of each bowl.

SALADS

✼

Fresh Baby Corn with Sherry Vinaigrette

SERVES 4

This recipe depends on its major ingredient, which depends in turn on your specialty grocer (in New York, Amazing Foods). Baby corn, so young that you eat it all, husk, kernels, and cob, is worth the hunt for it, even if you have to have it shipped in. It is all corn essence—so tender that I've given it the barest whisper of a dressing.

8 tiny fresh baby corn ears,
    husk on
2 perfect medium-size
    tomatoes, peeled
8 fresh basil sprigs
¼ cup sherry vinegar

1 teaspoon salt
1 good dash of Tabasco
1 teaspoon Dijon mustard
1 cup light olive oil

Trim larger husks from the outside of the corn ears; gently fold back the husks from the ear and pull away the silk. Pull the husks back gently to expose the ear, fanning the husks behind the ear and laying them out flat on the plate, two to a serving. Slice the tomatoes, then slice into halves and arrange two halves on each side of the corn fans. Decorate with basil sprigs.

Whisk together vinegar, salt, Tabasco, and mustard. Slowly drizzle the olive oil into the mixture, whisking constantly, until completely absorbed and lightly emulsified. Sprinkle over the corn husks and tomatoes. Serve at once, and don't forget to eat the basil.

Baby Green Beans and Corn

SERVES 6

3 cups fresh corn kernels
¼ cup balsamic vinegar
4 cups baby French green
  beans, called haricots
  verts
2 thick slices bacon, diced
  fine

Salt and pepper
1 bunch arugula and 1 bunch
  watercress, trimmed,
  washed, and dried

Toss corn kernels with vinegar and set aside. Bring 2 quarts of water to a boil; plunge green beans into water for 1 minute, then drain.

Fry the bacon over a medium flame until its fat is rendered, about 5 minutes. Remove bacon pieces and set aside. Toss corn with the hot bacon fat until just heated through. Add warm green beans and salt and pepper to taste. Lift lightly onto a bed of arugula and watercress.

MAIN COURSES

※

Grilled Tuna with Corn Relish

SERVES 4

Fresh tuna is one of the great gifts of Japanese culture and modern American chefs to our kitchen; until fifteen years ago, we had all our tuna from cans, and had no idea how wonderful fresh tuna was: firm, pungent, very good rare. The affinity of fresh tuna for corn was an unknown, too—but no longer. And please, please, even if you're unwilling to leave your tuna pink in the middle, don't for heaven's sake cook it past moist and flaky.

2 cups fresh corn kernels
½ cup fine-diced red bell pepper
½ cup fine-diced green bell pepper
1 small red onion, diced fine
¼ cup fine-diced celery
2 teaspoons ground cumin
1 tablespoon fine-chopped coriander

2 heavy dashes of Tabasco
A squeeze of lime juice
½ teaspoon grated lime zest
4 tuna steaks
1 cup virgin olive oil
Salt and pepper to taste
2 bunches arugula, washed and dried

Toss vegetables together with cumin, coriander, Tabasco, and lime juice and zest and let stand for at least 2 hours in the refrigerator. Dip tuna steaks in olive oil and grill over hot coals, about 4 minutes to the side, until outside is white and dark-striped and the center is alabaster-pink. Season with salt and pepper as you go.

Serve steaks on a bed of arugula, with the relish on or near them, and accompany with sliced beefsteak tomatoes and black beans.

Cheddar-Grits Soufflé with Smithfield Ham Sauce

SERVES 6

Those of us raised on grits (and we were raised on it mostly as a breakfast dish, with ham or sausage and eggs) are never secure unless it's on the kitchen shelf, ready to comfort us at a moment's notice. This dish combines the elegance and lightness of a soufflé with the homely taste of grits, and sneaks the ham into the sauce.

3 cups milk
2 tablespoons grits
4 tablespoons butter
4 tablespoons flour
Salt and pepper to taste
8 eggs, separated
1 cup fresh white corn
　　kernels
¼ pound sharp Cheddar
　　cheese, grated (about 1½
　　cups)

¼ cup grated Parmesan
　　cheese
Smithfield Ham and Peanut
　　Sauce (see following
　　recipe)
Chopped peanuts and
　　scallions, as garnish

Heat 1 cup of the milk in a small saucepan until scalded, then whisk in the grits and stir briskly until the grits is cooked, about 6 minutes. Set aside.

Melt butter in a heavy saucepan and whisk in the flour. Cook over low heat for 7 or 8 minutes, not letting the flour color. Add the remaining 2 cups milk a little at a time, beating all the time with a whisk. Add salt and pepper. Beat the egg yolks and add them, beating all the time, to the béchamel. Remove from heat, then stir in the room-temperature grits, the corn kernels, and the Cheddar cheese.

Butter the inside of a 3-quart soufflé dish and sprinkle with the Parmesan cheese, rotating the dish to coat evenly. Refrigerate. Preheat oven to 425° F.

Beat the egg whites until stiff; stir half of them into the egg yolk mixture; then fold the rest in slowly and gently. Pile the mixture into the chilled soufflé dish and put in the oven for 5 minutes. Lower the heat to 375° F and cook for another 30 minutes, or until crisp on the outside and moist at the center. Remember not to open the oven door before the 30-minute cooking time is up. Serve at once.

Spoon sauce over each serving of the soufflé, with a sprinkle of chopped peanuts and scallions.

Smithfield Ham and Peanut Sauce

2 tablespoons butter
1 medium onion, diced
1 cup Smithfield ham pieces
   (trimmings from the bone
   are fine or use the ready-
   to-serve Smithfield ham
   steaks in meat case)

1 cup roasted unsalted
   peanuts
2 cups chicken stock
1 cup heavy cream
1 teaspoon black pepper
1 heavy dash of Tabasco
1 cup coffee

Over a medium flame in a heavy skillet, sauté onion in butter until translucent; process along with ham and peanuts with the sharp blade in a food processor bowl, adding 1 cup of the chicken stock to moisten. Run until it forms a smooth paste, then add cream and turn off processor at once. Turn out into a bowl and add seasonings, stir, and then slowly add the coffee. Add remaining cup of chicken stock, continuing to stir until the sauce is the consistency of a light béchamel, a little heavier than heavy cream; add more chicken stock and cream if necessary.

DESSERTS

⊠

Corn Ice Cream with Parched Corn Caramel Sauce

SERVES 8

12 ears perfectly fresh new
  corn
2 quarts half-and-half
1 cup parched corn*
2 cups sugar

16 egg yolks
½ teaspoon salt
1 teaspoon vanilla extract
Parched Corn Caramel Sauce
  (see following recipe)

Husk corn and slice down the middle of each row of kernels, then cut kernels from the cobs, reserving 6 cobs. Be careful not to let any of the corn milk escape—slice the kernels off the cobs directly into a bowl. Bring the half-and-half to scalding and add the parched corn. Let seethe, just below a simmer, for about 20 minutes. Strain the half-and-half into another pan and reserve the parched corn, closely covered, for the sauce. Add the sugar and the corn kernels and their liquid and the reserved 6 corncobs to the half-and-half and let seethe for another 20 minutes. Meanwhile, beat the egg yolks until light yellow and sticky and add the salt and the vanilla.

Remove the corncobs and strain the half-and-half and corn through a fine sieve, pressing hard to force as much corn essence through as possible. Pour 2 cups of the half-and-half mixture over the egg yolks, whisking constantly; add the rest of the half-and-half mixture and continue to whisk. Return to the pan and once again bring almost to scalding, whisking constantly. Cool. Freeze in a rotary freezer and store at 0° F until firm. Serve with the sauce.

* Parched corn is air-dried fresh corn, processed and used mostly in Pennsylvania by the Amish. It's available by mail from Bird-in-Hand Country Bake Shop, R.D. 1, Gibbons Road, Bird-in-Hand, PA 17505.

Parched Corn Caramel Sauce

¼ cup heavy cream
1 cup softened parched corn
   reserved from the ice
   cream

2 cups sugar
4 tablespoons cold butter
Pinch of salt

Heat heavy cream to almost scalding and pour over parched corn. Melt sugar over low heat in a small heavy saucepan (do not stir). When dark brown, whisk in the cold butter in small bits, then whisk in the cream and parched corn. If the sauce is too thick, add a smidgen more cream. Add the salt. Serve warm or at room temperature over the corn ice cream.

Indian Pudding

SERVES 8

It's a sure thing that Indian pudding isn't Indian—molasses is a byproduct of rum making, which was not an Indian pursuit; the English introduced it to America, along with slavery. But the corn was all New World, and certainly this simple dessert tastes basic enough to have been one of the dishes at the earliest of Thanksgivings. It's still a treat.

5 cups milk	1 teaspoon salt
¼ cup cornmeal	¼ cup sugar
4 tablespoons butter	2 teaspoons cinnamon
½ cup unsulfured molasses	1¼ teaspoons powdered
3 eggs, beaten	ginger

Preheat oven to 250° F.

In a 2-quart saucepan, scald 3 cups of the milk; sprinkle the cornmeal into the milk, whisking constantly, then continue whisking until the mixture thickens and the cornmeal is soft. Stir in the butter. Beat together the molasses, eggs, salt, sugar, cinnamon, and ginger. Beat into the cornmeal mixture. Pour into a deep 2-quart baking dish and pour 1 cup of milk, cold, over the top. Do not stir. Bake for 3½ to 4 hours. When the cold milk is absorbed, stir the pudding from the bottom and add the remaining cup of milk.

Serve plain with heavy cream for breakfast or as a simple dessert.

For a fancier dessert, serve with vanilla, corn, or rum raisin ice cream on top. Or caramelize apples (see following recipe) and serve over pudding with whipped cream.

Caramelized Apples

4 tart apples

1 cup brown sugar

4 tablespoons butter

¼ teaspoon salt

Peel, core, and slice apples. Put sugar in a heavy 1-quart saucepan and melt over a low flame, not stirring. When sugar is melted, beat in butter and salt and add apples all at once. Toss the apples with the caramel over low heat until they soften, then continue cooking until apples are very soft, but have not fallen apart.

OTHER GOOD THINGS

Confetti Corn Bread

SERVES 8

This is everything–corn bread: Just about all the ingredients I've ever tried and liked in corn bread are in this version. It's best with simple meats and gravies that will serve as a complement to all this richness.

2 cups cornmeal
2 cups all-purpose flour
2 tablespoons baking powder
1 teaspoon salt
½ cup small-diced green and
    red bell peppers
½ cup small-diced celery
½ cup small-diced red onions

2 tablespoons fine-diced
    pickled jalapeños
1 cup fresh corn kernels
½ cup grated Cheddar cheese
4 cups milk
½ cup crumbled fried bacon
¼ cup soy oil or bacon grease

Preheat oven to 425° F.

Sift together cornmeal, flour, baking powder, and salt. Add vegetables and cheese and toss lightly. Add the milk and bacon and stir briskly to mix thoroughly.

In a 12-inch cast-iron skillet,* heat the oil or bacon fat to almost smoking; pour in the batter and transfer at once to oven. Bake for 25 minutes, or until the corn bread sounds hollow when tapped and a knife stuck in the center comes out clean. Turn out and serve at once. (Corn bread turns into a hockey puck about 5 minutes out of the oven. If you don't finish it at once, save it for stuffing.)

* I don't recommend trying this with anything but a cast-iron skillet. Cast-iron pots and pans are one of the great gifts of America to American cookery—once seasoned, they are sturdy, conduct heat beautifully, and are easy to care for. Try one —you'll never go back to anything lesser. Otherwise, use a good heavy baking pan and proceed as above, but do not let the oil get as hot; heat over a medium flame for about 4 minutes, then pour in the batter.

Corn Bread Stuffing

SERVES AT LEAST 8

This is what to do—and all you *can* do—with leftover corn bread, and it's especially good with the Confetti Corn Bread. I've added a fillip or two, but it's just as good with nothing but a little chicken stock to moisten, and then straight into the bird.

½ pound pork sausage meat
2 tablespoons butter
2 chicken livers, chopped fine
Chicken heart and gizzard,
  chopped fine
½ cup each fine-diced celery,
  onion, and green bell
  pepper
1 teaspoon chopped thyme
1 teaspoon chopped sage
½ teaspoon oregano

2 garlic cloves, chopped
1 recipe Confetti Corn Bread
  (see preceding recipe),
  roughly crumbled
4 hard-boiled eggs, chopped
Salt and pepper to taste
Tabasco to taste
1 teaspoon Worcestershire
  sauce
1 cup chicken stock

Put pork sausage into a hot cast-iron skillet a bit at a time and stir until it loses its color and begins to render its fat. Add the butter, then add livers, heart, and gizzard and cook just until they lose their red color. Add vegetables and herbs and garlic and cook until vegetables are limp. Toss this mixture with the crumbled corn bread. Add the hard-boiled eggs and toss. Stir in seasonings, then moisten with the chicken stock. (This makes a fairly loose stuffing, which is what I like best; if you want your stuffing to hold together more firmly, add 2 beaten eggs at this point.)

Stuff the bird (it will be more than enough for a chicken; and should fully stuff front and back cavities of a 20-pound turkey). Put any extra stuffing in a baking pan, drizzle with butter, and heat it for 20 minutes in a 400° F oven so you'll have extra (which I always need).

PUMPKINS

Pumpkins are jolly, seasonal, and underestimated. Maybe it's their innocent, quilted look, sitting orange and plump in New England in early autumn fields, ready for harvest, that makes us see them as a New England specialty—candidates mostly for pie baking. Recently, this one-note tune is changing. We're looking for inspiration to the New Mexicans, who've used pumpkin dozens of ways for years, and to the Italians, who came up with pumpkin pasta and a variety of pumpkin soups. The picture of those bouncy orange globes in countless autumn fields has conjured up dozens of new ideas for great dishes.

The New England way with pumpkin is intimately connected with the "pumpkin pie" spices—allspice, ginger, cinnamon, and cloves—and any pumpkin preparation that uses them is bound to conjure up pie, leaving the eater with an odd sense of dislocation: "Tastes like pumpkin pie. Looks like pumpkin pie. Where's the crust?" Pumpkin soups and main dishes do better when other flavorings are used, and we invite a whole new experience of the rich color and silky texture of the big squash.

It's important not to let pumpkin get bogged down: Cooked and mashed, it can be very heavy—it always wants lightening with cream or stock or eggs, or varying with meat or other vegetables. Like all the squashes, it is essentially bland and smooth, and so is the perfect background for stronger flavors and rougher textures.

The pumpkin shell is an ideal container: Small ones look beautiful filled with soup or custard, and large ones make great bakers for casseroles or desserts, the container becoming part of the dish.

SOME BASICS

The first thing to remember about pumpkin is not to be intimidated by the raw form of the thing—fresh pumpkin is better than canned pumpkin, and the whole pumpkin, large or small, becomes a charming serving piece for itself and other things, so don't be seduced by the can or put off by the squash.

How to Deal with a Raw Pumpkin

Cut the top off as for a jack-o'-lantern and slice the strings off the top piece with a knife. Using the sharp edge of a large metal spoon, scrape strings and seeds out of the body of the pumpkin: This is worth persevering in enough to be thorough, because seeds and strings are very unpleasant in cooked pumpkin and will depress you —they're almost impossible to separate from the pulp after this first step, so you might as well do it right the first time.

When you've scraped the inside really clean, separate the strings from the seeds and discard the strings, then wash and dry the seeds.

Toasted Pumpkin Seeds

Toss washed and dried seeds with soy oil or clarified butter, 4 cups of seeds to ½ cup fat. Put one layer deep on a sided cookie sheet and toast in a 350° F oven for about 20 minutes, until crisp and golden brown (larger seeds from the largest pumpkins may take 30 minutes). Season to taste with salt and pepper and whichever of the following appeals to you: cayenne, cumin, oregano, dried coriander, or dried cardamom. Use as a sprinkle on soups or stews or as a cocktail snack.

Cooked Pumpkin Pulp

FROM AN 8-INCH-DIAMETER PUMPKIN:
ABOUT 3 CUPS OF PURÉE

FROM A 12-INCH-DIAMETER PUMPKIN:
ABOUT 6 CUPS OF PURÉE

With a large chef's knife, cut the pumpkin into manageable chunks. Be careful—the knife should be sharp and your stroke firm, or the blade will slide off the tough skin and cut you. To be safest, drive the tip of the knife into the pumpkin skin and then use a downward stroke. Cut the strings and seeds from the pulp, then cut off the skin, then cut the pulp into smaller chunks (if you're going to reduce the pulp to purée, the smaller the better; otherwise, consider the size and texture of pieces you'll need for whatever recipe you're following).

Cover the bottom of a heavy saucepan large enough to hold all the pumpkin with water to about 2 inches in depth, then add the pumpkin chunks. Cover the pan and bring to a boil over a high flame, then reduce to medium and cook until all the pumpkin is tender to the mashing point, about 45 minutes. Turn the pumpkin gently from the bottom every 15 minutes, and add water if the pan shows signs of going dry.

Use a food processor to purée the cooked pulp, or proceed with the chunks as your recipe calls for.

SMALL PLATES

Savory Pumpkin Tarts

MAKES 8 TARTS

4 eggs
1½ cups puréed Cooked
    Pumpkin Pulp (page 82)
2 cups cream
1 large onion, small-diced
4 tablespoons butter
2 teaspoons chopped fresh
    thyme

2 teaspoons chopped fresh
    rosemary
1 teaspoon cayenne
1 teaspoon salt
Cayenne-Cheddar Pastry (see
    following recipe)
1 cup grated Parmesan cheese

Preheat oven to 375° F.

Beat eggs and fold in the beaten purée and heavy cream. Season to taste with salt and pepper. Sauté onion in butter until translucent and ivory-colored. Add thyme, rosemary, cayenne, and salt and cook until herbs are limp. Let cool.

Roll out pastry and cut into 5-inch rounds. Line 4-inch tart pans with rounds and brush with beaten egg whites.

Spread onion mixture over the bottom of each tart shell. Top with pumpkin custard, sprinkle with Parmesan cheese, and bake for about 20 minutes, until pastry is golden and custard just set.

Cayenne-Cheddar Pastry

2 cups all-purpose flour
1½ teaspoons salt
1½ teaspoons cayenne
¼ pound plus 3 tablespoons
butter

¼ cup grated sharp Cheddar
cheese
3 tablespoons ice water

Sift flour, salt, and cayenne together and work butter into the mixture with two knives or a pastry blender until it is about the texture of cornmeal. Toss with Cheddar cheese and add the water, mixing lightly with a fork until the dry mixture just holds together. Press together into a ball and chill for 30 minutes.

Spicy Meatballs with Pumpkin Sauce

MAKES 24 TO 30 MEATBALLS;
8 APPETIZER SERVINGS,
6 AS A MAIN COURSE

THE MEATBALLS
2 cups soft fine breadcrumbs
1 cup milk
1 pound ground veal
1 pound ground pork
2 tablespoons chopped fresh
    coriander
1 tablespoon chopped oregano
2 teaspoons cayenne

2 teaspoons salt
2 teaspoons black pepper
½ teaspoon ground allspice
2 medium onions, minced
1 large red bell pepper,
    minced
2 large eggs

THE SAUCE
2 tablespoons soy oil
2 tablespoons ground cumin
1 cup dried ancho chile purée

4 cups puréed Cooked
    Pumpkin Pulp (page 82)
2 cups chicken stock
Salt and pepper to taste

Preheat oven to 400° F.

For the meatballs, combine breadcrumbs with milk. Combine all other ingredients, mix in softened breadcrumbs thoroughly, then form into small balls, 1 inch in diameter. Bake the meatballs on sided cookie sheets for about 25 minutes, until brown.

For the sauce, heat soy oil and add cumin. Stir, then add ancho purée. Whisk in pumpkin purée, then chicken stock, and stir to sauce consistency. Season with salt and pepper.

To serve as an hors d'oeuvre, put sauce in a bowl and surround with meatballs. Garnish with fresh coriander leaves.

To serve as a first course, place 6 meatballs on small plates and lay a broad stripe of sauce across them. Sprinkle with toasted pumpkin seeds and garnish with fresh coriander leaves.

SOUPS

⁂

Cream of Pumpkin with Cardamom

SERVES 8

1 large onion, diced
2 tablespoons butter
2 teaspoons ground
   cardamom
1 teaspoon cayenne
1 teaspoon ground oregano

Salt and pepper to taste
2 cups puréed Cooked
   Pumpkin Pulp (page 82)
2 quarts chicken stock
Toasted pumpkin seeds
   (pepitas), for garnish

Sauté diced onion in butter and add cardamom, cayenne, oregano, salt, and pepper. Sauté until onion is translucent. Stir in pumpkin purée, then whisk in chicken stock a little at a time, until perfectly smooth. Simmer to marry flavors, then strain and serve with toasted pumpkin seeds on top.

Cold Pumpkin-Orange Soup

SERVES 8

3 cups puréed Cooked
  Pumpkin Pulp (page 82)
1 quart fresh orange juice
2 teaspoons fine-grated
  orange zest

2 ounces fresh ginger
1 pint Gewurtztraminer
Thin-sliced unpeeled oranges,
  for garnish

Whisk purée until smooth; boil all other ingredients together for 5 minutes and strain. Whisk into purée. Chill and serve with thin-sliced oranges for garnish.

SALADS

※

Warm Pumpkin Salad
on Watercress

SERVES 4

2 tablespoons soy oil
2 cups raw pumpkin slices,
  2 x 3 inches
1 cup red bell pepper slices
½ cup thin-sliced quartered
  fresh pineapple
½ teaspoon hot pepper flakes
2 tablespoons soy sauce

2 tablespoons sliced scallions,
  green and white parts
½ cup Gewurtztraminer
1 tablespoon sherry vinegar
2 bunches watercress
1 ounce pickled ginger, or
  about 12 slices

Heat soy oil to very hot in a wok. Add pumpkin and red pepper and toss lightly for about 1 minute. Add pineapple, then quite quickly pepper flakes, ginger, soy sauce, and scallions. Toss again, then add wine and sherry vinegar and cook just until liquid is almost evaporated. Serve on a nest of watercress, garnished with ginger.

Autumn Salad

SERVES 4

1 cup ½-inch pumpkin cubes,
  very lightly steamed
1 cup crisp unpeeled
  Northern Spy apple cubes
1 cup ripe unpeeled Bosc pear
  cubes
1 cup diced fennel
1 cup chopped dried peaches,
  slightly plumped in hot
  water

½ cup Poppy Seed Dressing
  (see below)
4 cups fine-sliced red cabbage
  or torn chicory, or a
  mixture of the two

Toss everything together and serve on a tangle of sliced red cabbage or chicory.

Poppy Seed Dressing

MAKES 2½ CUPS

½ cup extra-fine sugar
1 tablespoon dry mustard
2 teaspoons salt
⅔ cup cider vinegar
3 tablespoons grated onion
  (about 1 onion)

2 cups soy, corn, or peanut
  oil—not olive oil
3 tablespoons poppy seeds

Stir together sugar, mustard, salt, and vinegar. Add grated onion and stir thoroughly. Add oil in a long drizzle, whisking constantly, and continue to beat until thick. Add poppy seeds and beat for a few seconds longer. Store in a cool place.

MAIN COURSES

Sausage-Stuffed Pumpkin

SERVES 10

1 pumpkin, about 14 inches
in diameter
Salt and black pepper
2 teaspoons ground allspice
2 pounds pork sausage meat
1 large Spanish onion, diced
3 celery ribs, diced
2 tablespoons chopped fresh
parsley
1 tablespoon dried thyme
1 teaspoon rubbed sage
4 garlic cloves, minced
1 teaspoon cayenne
4 large firm apples, Ida Reds
or Romes, peeled, cored,
and diced

4 Bosc pears, peeled, cored,
and diced
½ cup reduced cider*
1 teaspoon orange zest
1 tablespoon balsamic
vinegar
½ cup brown sugar
¼ pound butter
2 cups pecan meats
2 cups fine-chopped scallions,
for garnish

Prepare pumpkin for stuffing by cleaning (page 80). Rub inside with 1 tablespoon salt, 2 teaspoons pepper, and allspice.

Preheat oven to 400° F.

Heat a skillet to medium heat and crumble sausage meat into it. Add onion and celery, parsley, thyme, sage, garlic, cayenne, 2 teaspoons black pepper, and 2 teaspoons salt. Sauté until sausage is beginning to brown and onion is transparent.

Toss apples, pears, orange juice, orange zest, vinegar, and brown sugar together. Melt 4 tablespoons of the butter in a heavy skillet until it foams, then add pecans and 1 teaspoon salt and toss. Transfer skillet to oven and brown pecans lightly; it should take about 10 minutes. Reduce oven heat to 350° F.

Fill the pumpkin with layers of sausage, fruit, and pecans, in that order, repeating as needed but ending with fruit. Top with the remaining 4 tablespoons butter and put the lid on the pumpkin. Set it in a roasting pan in 2 inches of water and bake at 350° F for about 2½ hours, or until it begins to turn brown and cave in slightly.

Remove pumpkin from pan, using two spatulas to keep the bottom intact. Transfer to a large round platter.

To serve, remove pumpkin lid and scoop out contents with a large spoon, sprinkling each serving with chopped scallions.

* To reduce cider: Boil 4 cups of cider in a nonreactive pan until reduced to ½ cup.

Winter-Light Stew

SERVES 10

8 cups chicken stock
1 bay leaf
4 fresh sage leaves
2 fresh thyme branches
1 pound white turnips, peeled and sliced
1 pound pumpkin, peeled and cut into 1 x 1½-inch pieces
1 bunch mustard greens

2 large leeks, sliced and well cleaned of sand
4 tablespoons butter
1 tablespoon salt
2 teaspoons black pepper
2 pounds boneless, skinless turkey pieces, thigh and breast
Sliced scallions, for garnish

Bring chicken stock to a boil with bay leaf and herbs. Lower to a simmer and add turnips; cook until almost tender, about 15 minutes. Add pumpkin and chopped mustard greens and cook another 10 minutes.

Meanwhile, in a 2-gallon Dutch oven sauté leek slices in butter with salt and pepper. When limp, add turkey pieces and toss everything together. When turkey becomes opaque, add chicken stock mixture to leeks and turkey and simmer to marry flavors, about 15 minutes. Do not cook longer, or turkey will be rubbery.

Serve in soup bowls with sprinkles of scallion.

DESSERTS

Miriam Ungerer's Pumpkin Mousse Pie

SERVES 12

This is the perfect pumpkin pie—rich and deep, but light enough to eat seconds. I'd never gotten the pumpkin pie I hoped for until Phoebe, Ms. Ungerer's daughter, came to cook desserts for us. This pie is both rich and light, full of good spice flavors and deep with pumpkinness.

Butter Pastry (page 53)
1 tablespoon plus 1 teaspoon unflavored gelatin
¼ cup cold water
4 eggs, separated
½ cup heavy cream
½ cup milk
2 cups puréed Cooked Pumpkin Pulp (page 82)
1 cup brown sugar, not *packed*
¼ teaspoon each cinnamon, nutmeg, ground ginger
Pinch of ground cloves
¼ cup white sugar
1 tablespoon bourbon or cognac
½ cup black walnuts, chopped, for garnish
1 cup heavy cream, whipped, for garnish

Roll out pastry and line a 10-inch pie plate with it. Line pastry with foil and weight with beans. Bake at 425° F till brown, about 15 minutes. Let cool.

Sprinkle the gelatin over cold water. In the top of a double boiler or a very heavy nonaluminum saucepan beat the egg yolks until light, then beat in cream, milk, and half of the pumpkin purée.

Beat in the brown sugar and spices, then cook, stirring constantly, over low heat or in the top of a double boiler until mixture becomes a thick custard. Remove from heat and stir in gelatin and remaining pumpkin, making certain it is smoothly incorporated.

Cool to tepid. Set custard pan into a pan half filled with ice and water and stir the custard about 5 minutes.

Beat egg whites fairly stiff, adding white sugar last. Add bourbon or cognac, then fold into custard with a rubber spatula. Scrape into pastry shell and chill at least two hours. Sprinkle with walnuts and garnish with whipped cream.

Sweet Stuffed Pumpkin

SERVES 8

1 pumpkin, about 12 inches
   in diameter
2 tablespoons cinnamon
1 teaspoon ground cloves
1½ cups brown sugar
1 cup orange juice, with 1
   teaspoon orange zest
8 peeled, cored, and diced
   firm sweet apples, Rome or
   Ida Red

8 peeled, cored, and diced
   Bosc pears
1 cup toasted pecan pieces
2 cups raisins
2 tablespoons butter
2 cups heavy cream

Preheat oven to 375° F.

Prepare pumpkin for stuffing (page 80). Rub inside of the pumpkin with 2 teaspoons cinnamon, ½ teaspoon ground cloves, and ½ cup brown sugar. Toss orange juice and zest with apples and pears; add remaining sugar and spices. Mix nuts and raisins.

Layer raisins and nuts with apples and pears inside the pumpkin, ending with fruit. When filled, top with butter and the pumpkin lid. Put pumpkin in a roasting pan and cover bottom of pan with water to a depth of 1 inch.

Bake 2½ hours, until pumpkin begins to turn brown and cave in slightly. Scoop out fruit and pumpkin; serve with heavy cream.

TOMATOES

I t's not, heaven knows, that only Americans like tomatoes: The Italians have based a whole series of regional cuisines on them. And the further south one goes in France, the more one sees tomatoes in food preparation (that's why I like Provençal cooking better than Burgundian). But it is true that we use tomatoes constantly and ubiquitously, and that our tomatoes can be among the best in the world. We've adapted tomato sauce from the Italians; we've made ketchup our national relish, taking it from the English; and we've invented and reinvented the fresh, raw tomato, coming to it anew every summer and eating it with steaks, with corn on the cob, in salads, and chopped as a sauce.

It's well to remember a couple of things about tomatoes: Canned tomatoes can be wonderful, a really good way to get through winter, the mainstay of dozens of sauces and soups and main dishes. Fresh vine-ripened tomatoes are a delicacy comparable only to young as-paragus in the spring—but beware of the chilled, unripe, pinky-white tomatoes raised by agribusiness and shipped year-round all over the United States. They are good for nothing. They take up the space that other—any other—foods could occupy, and they make us forget how wonderful real tomatoes are.

The vine-ripened tomato is available in most parts of the country from mid-July through September. It is firm but very juicy, and when dead ripe goes very slightly soft; the soft ones are better for sauces than for slicing. At its best, the fruit comes straight from the vine where it's grown—it shouldn't be refrigerated until just before it's due to be served, and in fact is better served at room temperature without chilling. But if you insist on a cold salad, then put it in the refrigerator only an hour or so before slicing. The best way to have fresh tomatoes in season is to grow them, and a lot of Americans do, but if you develop a relationship with a market gardener, you'll be able to find out just where he delivers in your town, and when, so that you'll know when to hotfoot over for a steady supply all summer. Better yet, find him where he lives and get your tomatoes at the source. It's worth the trip. Not everyone even bothers to slice a fresh tomato at its peak. My friend Parker's grandfather ate them out of hand, sprinkling with sugar as he went. Try it.

As for green tomatoes, if you grow your own you'll have a supply even sooner than you'll have red tomatoes. When a tomato is full grown, but not yet showing even a tinge of pink, it's ready to fry or chop for pies; usually end-of-season, post-frost green tomatoes are used for relish, mincemeat, or bottled pie filling. In the south, green tomatoes appear in the market late in the season, but in other regions you may have to talk your market gardener into bringing them to you specially. There isn't anything quite like their pungent, citrusy, fresh taste.

It is a tribute to our passion for this fruit that we overcame so soon our native suspicion of the strange—as late as the 1820s tomatoes were still considered poison, and, like many poisons, aphrodisiac. A hundred years later, they were one of the anchors of the American kitchen. Treasure them.

SMALL PLATES

Freshest Possible
Tomato Sauce

SERVES 4 AS A FIRST COURSE;
TO SERVE AS A LIGHT MAIN COURSE,
DOUBLE THE RECIPE

Most Americans were raised on some version of canned tomato sauce, and a lot of them are very good; but in high summer this is the one to use, forsaking all others.

2 tablespoons extra-virgin
    olive oil
3 tomatoes, peeled and diced
2 large parsley sprigs,
    chopped fine
6 large basil leaves, chopped
    fine

1 garlic clove, minced
Salt and pepper to taste
½ pound fresh linguine or
    fettuccine
Basil leaves, for garnish
1 cup freshly grated Romano
    cheese

Set 1 gallon of water to boil. Just as it comes to a needle boil, heat olive oil in a 12-inch cast-iron skillet until a bit of bread dropped into it browns at once. Add the tomatoes to the olive oil and simmer briefly to combine. Add parsley, basil, garlic, salt, and pepper. Cook gently just until herbs go limp. Remove from flame.

By now the water will be at a full boil; toss in the pasta and cook for 2 minutes. Drain, then toss with 2 tablespoons of sauce. Serve on a round platter topped with the rest of the sauce and a garnish of fresh basil leaves. Pass Romano cheese with the pasta.

Sliced Summer Tomatoes
with Variations

*4 large vine-ripened
tomatoes, cooled but not
chilled, sliced thick*

Serve alone, unadorned, lightly seasoned with salt and pepper.

VARIATIONS

Chopped fresh basil and a drizzle of virgin olive oil, garnished with whole basil leaves.

Sliced smoked or fresh mozzarella, plus the above olive oil and basil.

Sprinkled with orange, lemon, grapefruit, or lime zest, a sprinkle of the juice, and sprigs of coriander.

Alternate tomato slices with orange slices, chopped rosemary, thyme, basil, oregano, and sliced niçoise olives, with extra-virgin olive oil, then shavings of prosciutto, wild-boar prosciutto,* or un- cooked American country ham, alone or with any of the herbs men- tioned above, with a generous grinding of fresh pepper.

Two ears of roasted or boiled fresh sweet corn.

A vinaigrette of five parts extra-virgin olive oil to one part balsamic vinegar, mustard, salt, and pepper. Toss the vinaigrette with slivers of red, green, yellow, orange, and purple bell peppers; or with blanched *haricots verts* (tiny green beans); or with crumbled blue cheese or bacon or chopped fresh herbs or anchovies or minced green or black olives or garlic or minced mixed vegetables: celery, fennel, peppers, red onions, and peeled broccoli stems.

A bed of mixed greens dressed with any of the vinaigrette variations above.

* Wild-boar prosciutto is available from Noel Perrin at the Texas Wild Game Co- operative, P.O. Box 530, Ingram, TX 78025.

Tomato-Vegetable Sauté

SERVES 4

This is summer perfection. I see no reason not to lunch on this dish in one of its variations two or three times a week all season. Sprinkle it with cheese, or grill a chicken breast or a bit of fresh tuna to go with it if you like, but just go on with this in some form and you'll have great memories to get you through the winter.

6 tablespoons unsalted butter
1 small onion, minced
4 medium-size ripe tomatoes, peeled and diced
Salt and pepper

2 cups any of the following: green beans, sliced and blanched for 2 minutes; haricots verts, *blanched for 2 minutes; broccoli florets and medallions, blanched for 2 minutes; fresh corn, cut from cob; fresh sweet peas; thin-sliced summer squash or zucchini*

Melt butter in a 2-quart heavy saucepan. Add minced onion and sauté until onion is transparent. Add tomato and toss with salt and fresh pepper. Simmer another 3 or 4 minutes to blend flavors, then toss vegetables with the tomatoes and let remain over heat just long enough to heat everything through. Serve at once as a first course or as a side dish.

Fried Green Tomatoes

SERVES 4

Tomatoes are a passion that Americans and Italians share; almost everyone else at least *likes* them. But green tomatoes are a strictly American preoccupation: firm, citrusy, almost chartreuse, they figure in recipes that are entirely our own, idiosyncratic enough never to be mistaken for anyone else's.

3 cups cornmeal	¼ pound butter, clarified, or
2 teaspoons salt	½ cup bacon grease or ½
1 teaspoon black pepper	cup vegetable oil
4 large green tomatoes, sliced	

Toss together cornmeal, salt, and pepper; dredge green tomato slices in cornmeal. Heat fat in a cast-iron skillet until it almost smokes. Fry the tomato slices quickly on both sides, arrange quickly on four individual plates, and garnish with chopped scallions, red tomatoes, or parsley.

THE TOMATO SANDWICH

One late fall in Berkshire County, Massachusetts, we were having our first great post-summer feast—pork roast, apple sauce, roots—when Steven Grob, who has great liquid black eyes and quite a line in doleful looks, suddenly looked especially doleful. "I just realized that I went all summer and never had a fresh tomato sandwich." We were all suitably stricken for him, knowing we couldn't do a thing; the last tomato vines had been plowed under weeks before. Don't let this happen to you. Keep tomatoes and mayonnaise and good bread in your kitchen all summer.

Not usually a first course in America, the tomato sandwich is, year in and year out, the perfect summer lunch. It is at its most beautiful in its purest form, but the addition of bacon creates that other American classic, the BLT. Cottony winter tomatoes turn this great sandwich into a dreary diner standard. Some of the variations given here *are* first courses, though, or hors d'oeuvres in smaller versions.

Basic and Beautiful

2 tablespoons mayonnaise,
  homemade (see following
  recipe) or Hellmann's
2 slices good white or whole
  wheat bread, or Cheddar
  bread

3 medium-thick slices
  summer tomato, peeled
Salt and pepper to taste
2 lettuce leaves, trimmed of
  ribs: Boston, romaine, or
  iceberg

Spread mayonnaise on both slices of bread. Lay tomatoes overlapping on one slice and season with salt and pepper. Add overlapping leaves of lettuce and top with second slice of bread. Bread may be toasted, but the softness of untoasted white bread chimes beautifully with the ripe tomato and the creamy mayonnaise. If the tomato is dead ripe and perfect, it is possible even to give up the mayonnaise, but no one would recommend such a course except in extreme cases of dietary necessity.

FOR A BLT
Add 2 or 3 slices of crisp, but not overcooked, bacon between the lettuce and the tomato.

ANOTHER CLASSIC
Add Cheddar cheese to the tomato or to the BLT.

Homemade Mayonnaise

MAKES 2½ CUPS

The paprika makes this a very American mayo; for that reason, it shouldn't taste strongly of olive oil, so use soy oil or a very light-flavored olive oil.

2 egg yolks
2 cups light olive oil or
   salad oil

Juice of ½ lemon
Salt and pepper to taste
1½ teaspoons paprika

Beat egg yolks until thick and lemony in color. Beat in oil, one drop at a time, until it begins to be assimilated; then pour in a very fine stream, beating all the while. When all the oil is absorbed, add lemon juice, salt, pepper, and paprika.

The Tomato Melt

The perfect way to combine cheese with tomato, the melt is infinitely variable, fresh-tasting, and rich in all its versions; the cheese melts, but the tomato should not cook.

2 slices good white or whole
   wheat bread
1 tablespoon soft butter and
   1 tablespoon spicy brown
   mustard, combined, or
   equal parts mayonnaise
   and Dijon mustard

4 thinnish slices peeled ripe
   summer tomatoes
Salt and pepper to taste
1 cup grated sharp Cheddar
   cheese

Toast bread on both sides; spread each slice with butter or mayonnaise mixture. Lay 2 slices of tomato overlapping on each slice and season with salt and pepper. Pack each slice with grated Cheddar, to a thickness of about ½ inch, being sure to cover tomato slices completely, and the bread right to the edge.

Slide sandwich under a broiler at medium flame, or into a toaster oven set at 400° F, top only. Cook for 12 to 15 minutes, until cheese is melted and beginning to bubble at the edges. Serve at once.

VARIATIONS

Use dark or light rye bread and caraway or dill Havarti cheese.

Sprinkle chopped onion or garlic between tomato and cheese.

Omit mustard and spread bread with a heavily herbed butter.

Lay a thin slice of ham between cheese and tomato, or top with 2 slices of hot bacon as it comes from the broiler.

Substitute garlic or hot-pepper jelly for butter or mayonnaise mixture.

Use French or Italian bread, rub with olive oil instead of butter or mayonnaise. Top with garlic, chopped basil, and provolone cheese.

Bruschetti

SERVES 2 AS A LUNCHEON SANDWICH,
OR 4 AS A FIRST COURSE

This is the Italian version of the tomato sandwich, just as the pizza is the Italian version of the melt. Lighter than the LT or the BLT, and open faced, it makes an exquisite summer first course.

2 slices day-old French or
Italian bread, or 1 Italian
roll, split and slightly
hollowed out
2 garlic cloves
2 medium-size summer
tomatoes

2 large parsley sprigs
6 large basil leaves
2 tablespoons extra-virgin
olive oil
Salt and pepper to taste

Split one of the garlic cloves and rub it on the bread or roll. Place in a 350° F oven to warm while you mince garlic; peel and dice tomatoes; fine-chop parsley and basil. Toss everything together with the olive oil and pile loosely on the bread or into the roll. Let stand 5 or 10 minutes before serving. Garnish with whole basil leaves.

VARIATIONS

Add 1 teaspoon chopped rosemary, thyme, and oregano and 3 thin-sliced niçoise olives. Mash ½ anchovy into olive oil.

Add ½ cup small cubes of smoked or fresh mozzarella or provolone cheese, or a heaping tablespoon of freshly grated Parmesan or Romano.

Add ½ cup Genoa salami or Black Forest ham cut into tiny cubes.

Add ½ cup cubed fresh poached or smoked turkey or chicken breast.

SOUPS

✄

Tomato Essence

SERVES 8

This is the purest of all tomato soups, and it's no accident that it's a Shaker recipe. The Shakers were farm cooks, growers and sellers of culinary and medicinal herbs, and great believers in simple treatment of fine ingredients.

4 tablespoons unsalted butter
4 celery ribs, diced
1 onion, diced
10 large basil leaves, with
    stems
2 parsley sprigs
2 thyme sprigs
1 small oregano sprig
2 teaspoons salt

½ teaspoon Tabasco
1 teaspoon black pepper
1 short lemon zest curl
2 quarts very ripe summer
    tomatoes, fine-chopped
1 cup heavy cream, whipped
    and salted
8 or 10 basil leaves in
    julienne

Melt butter in a heavy 3-quart nonreactive saucepan. Add celery, onion, herbs, seasonings, and the lemon zest. Simmer for 20 minutes, until vegetables are very soft. Add tomatoes and simmer for another 30 minutes, until tomatoes have fallen apart and have released all their liquid.

Run through a food mill or fine-mesh sieve. Reheat briefly and serve with salted whipped cream and fresh basil leaves.

Corn, Tomato, and Bacon Soup

SERVES 8

Tomatoes and corn are a combination that almost any American will find familiar; I noticed when I was reading for this book that tomatoes kept popping up in the corn chapters and corn in the tomato chapters of every book I looked at on American cooking. We are onto a good thing here.

1 quart chicken stock
1 ham hock
2 slices bacon
1 large onion, small-diced
3 tablespoons chopped
  parsley
3 basil leaves, chopped

1 bay leaf
2 cups fresh or canned corn
  kernels, with juice
3 cups fine-chopped peeled
  fresh or canned tomatoes
Salt and pepper to taste
Chopped parsley, for garnish

Simmer stock with ham hock for 1 hour. Fry the bacon in a heavy nonreactive 1-gallon pot. When brown, remove bacon from pot and drain; set aside. In the bacon fat, sauté the onion until transparent, then add the herbs and corn and sauté for 5 minutes more. Add tomatoes and simmer for about 20 minutes, or until all ingredients are well blended. Remove ham hock from chicken stock and add stock to soup. Season with salt and pepper and garnish with reserved bacon, crumbled, and chopped parsley.

MAIN DISHES

⊠

Grilled Chicken Breast and Eggplant with Baked Tomatoes

SERVES 6

4 lemons
2½ cups extra-virgin olive oil
8 garlic cloves
1 bunch basil
½ bunch parsley
2 cups white wine
6 whole chicken breasts,
   skinned, boned, and
   trimmed

6 medium-size firm, ripe
   summer tomatoes, peeled
6 longitudinal slices peeled
   eggplant
Salt and pepper to taste

Grate the zest of 2 of the lemons. Strip the zest from the other two in long curls. Make a marinade for the chicken breasts with 2 cups olive oil, 4 of the garlic cloves, two thirds of the basil and parsley, chopped, the lemon juice, the zest, and white wine. They should rest in the marinade in a nonreactive container for 2 or more hours.

Thirty minutes before serving time, purée remaining garlic, basil, grated lemon zest, and parsley together with ⅓ cup of the remaining olive oil. Preheat oven to 400° F. Cut tomatoes in half, sprinkle with remaining olive oil, salt, and pepper, and set in oven. Bake for 15 minutes.

Heat grill to hot. Lift out marinated breasts, shaking to rid them of excess oil. Grill for about 4 minutes to the side, or until they're just past pink at the center. Set aside in a warm place and dip the eggplant into the chicken marinade. Grill about 3 minutes to the side, until dark-striped outside and tender inside. Lay eggplant spoke-fashion on a large round platter and put a chicken breast on each one. Set the baked tomato halves between the spokes and spread each with the basil-garlic purée. Serve at once.

Swiss Steak

SERVES 4 TO 6

This is a much-maligned and completely misnamed midwestern dish that tastes wonderful. It lightens long winters, is as good a way of tenderizing a tough piece of meat as any, and is deeply flavorful.

¼ pound suet
2 pounds bottom round or
   trimmed boneless chuck, 2
   inches thick
2 cups flour
1½ teaspoons salt
1 teaspoon black pepper
1 large onion, diced
1 green bell pepper, diced
2 celery ribs, diced
1 large carrot, diced

1 teaspoon dried basil
1 bay leaf
1 teaspoon dried thyme
1 tablespoon Worcestershire
   sauce
2 good dashes of Tabasco
3 cups beef stock
3 cups chopped canned
   tomatoes and juice
3 tablespoons chopped
   parsley

Roughly chop suet. In a 1-gallon heavy nonreactive Dutch oven or deep-sided skillet, render the suet until brown. Lift suet from rendered fat.

Dredge meat in flour seasoned with salt and pepper. Pound firmly to tenderize meat and combine its surface with the flour—use a meat mallet, a wine bottle, or the side of a saucer.

Brown the meat on both sides in the rendered beef fat, letting it become golden brown but being careful not to burn the surface or any flour that might come off in the fat. Remove meat from pot and set aside. Add vegetables, herbs, salt and pepper, Worcestershire, and Tabasco to the pan and simmer until onion is transparent. Add beef stock and tomatoes and simmer 5 minutes more. Return meat to the pot, submerging it completely by about 2 inches. Cover and simmer for 1 hour or so, until meat is fork-tender.

Lift meat out of pot and skim any excess fat from sauce; add parsley and stir.

Serve with buttered egg noodles, rice, or mashed potatoes.

Janet Swain's Lasagne

SERVES 8 TO 10

This is a very American lasagne, based on that good canned tomato sauce aforementioned. The trick here is the zucchini, not cooked at all really, just dropped into the hot sauce a few minutes before it goes between the pasta layers.

THE SAUCE

4 tablespoons butter
1/4 cup olive oil
2 onions, diced
1 large green bell pepper, diced
4 celery ribs, diced
2 carrots, diced
2 tablespoons chopped fresh parsley
1 tablespoon dried basil
2 teaspoons dried thyme
1 teaspoon dried oregano
2 bay leaves

6 garlic cloves, minced
1 tablespoon Worcestershire sauce
1/2 pound green beans, cut into thirds
1/2 pound mushrooms, sliced
2 quarts canned plum tomatoes, with juice, chopped
1 pint canned tomato sauce
3 cups diced zucchini
Salt and pepper to taste

THE LASAGNE

1 pound fresh green lasagne
1 pound whole-milk mozzarella

1 pound fresh ricotta cheese
1/2 pound fresh-grated Parmesan cheese

For the sauce, in a nonreactive pot melt butter in hot olive oil over a medium flame. Sauté onions, pepper, celery, and carrots in oil and butter. Add the herbs and garlic and Worcestershire sauce, then the mushrooms and beans. Sauté briefly. Add the tomatoes and sauce and simmer for 40 minutes to 1 hour. Add zucchini, stir in, and remove from fire. Season with salt and pepper.

Preheat oven to 425° F.

For the lasagne, bring a gallon of salted water to a boil. Dribble sauce in a thin layer on the bottom of a 9 x 12-inch roasting pan 3 inches deep. Drop 1/4 pound of the lasagne noodles into the boiling water for 1½ minutes. Remove noodles with tongs and lay out to line the pan. Spoon sauce over noodles, then top with mozzarella slices and spread with ricotta. Repeat the process with the rest of the noodles, using one quarter of them for each layer, ending with a layer of cheese. Sprinkle the top with Parmesan and bake for about 25 minutes, or until the pan bubbles and the Parmesan is brown.

Baked Red Snapper with Tomato-Crabmeat Sauce

SERVES 4

4 8-ounce red snapper fillets, boned and skinned
Salt and pepper to taste
Juice and grated zest of 1 lime
½ cup dry white wine
4 tablespoons melted butter
1 tablespoon light olive oil
½ medium sweet green pepper, minced
4 fresh ripe tomatoes, peeled, cored, and chopped

1 small clove garlic, minced
2 tblsp. chopped fresh basil
1 tblsp. chopped fresh thyme
Juice and grated zest of ½ lemon
2 teaspoons Worcestershire
3 good dashes Tabasco
2 tablespoons chopped parsley
8 ounces lump crabmeat, picked over
Lime slices and basil leaves

Preheat oven to 425° F.

Arrange snapper fillets on a sided cookie sheet. Mix salt, pepper, lime juice and zest, white wine, and 2 tablespoons melted butter and pour over fillets. Bake for about twenty minutes.

Heat the oil over medium flame and add butter. Saute green pepper; add tomatoes, garlic, and herbs and simmer five minutes. Add lemon juice, zest, salt, pepper, Worcestershire and Tabasco. Let sauce stand until fish is done, then remove fish from oven and reheat sauce; add parsley and crabmeat and toss just enough to heat the crabmeat.

Top fish with sauce; garnish with lime slices and basil leaves.

DESSERTS

Canadians eat their tomatoes sliced with sugar on them; that is, they treat them as a fruit. The only desserts we normally make with tomatoes are green-tomato desserts, and it's hard to find them outside the southern and midwestern homes they're cooked in. I've invented one ripe tomato dessert because I couldn't resist the idea. See how you like it.

Green Tomato Pie

SERVES 8

Cornflour Pastry for a
   double-crust pie (page 37)
6 large green tomatoes

2 cups brown sugar
2 teaspoons grated lemon zest
Pinch of ground cloves
2 tablespoons flour

Preheat oven to 375° F.

Roll out pastry and cut half for lattice strips. Line a 10-inch pie plate with the other half. Peel and dice tomatoes and toss with the brown sugar, zest, and cloves. Sprinkle the bottom of the pie shell with flour and pile the green tomatoes in the pan. Do a crisscross pattern with the pastry strips, and bake for 45 minutes. Put an aluminum-foil collar around the rim of the pie and turn the heat to 425° F; bake for another 15 minutes, until crust is golden brown and filling is bubbling.

Tomato Sherbet with Green Tomato Sauce

MAKES 2 CUPS

6 large dead-ripe tomatoes
2 cups white sugar
Juice and grated zest of 2
    lemons
2 ounces grated fresh ginger

THE SAUCE
3 large green tomatoes
2 cups brown sugar
Pinch of ground cloves

With a very sharp knife, chop the tomatoes, being very careful not to lose any of the juice. In a nonreactive pan, heat the tomatoes together with the sugar, lemon juice, zest, and ginger. Cook until the sugar is completely melted and the ginger is well incorporated. Cool to room temperature and strain through a chinoise or fine-mesh sieve. Freeze in a rotary freezer or an electric sorbet maker.

For the sauce, chop green tomatoes. Simmer in a nonreactive pan with the sugar, the cloves, and 1 cup water. Cook for about 1 hour, replacing the water as needed. The texture should be pourable but thick. When the tomatoes have been reduced almost to a liquid, remove from heat and cool briefly; strain through a chinoise or fine-mesh sieve and chill. Serve in a pool on a glass plate with a scoop or two of the sherbet on top.

SWEET POTATOES

⬚

We have the sweet potato from two sources: For Africans, the yam is a staple, and African-Americans brought their taste for it here, along with greens and okra and a variety of beans; yams developed here as well as in Africa and Asia. South America is the home of the sweet potato, too, which is what we normally eat and which we often call a yam. They are actually unrelated vegetables, though they may be used interchangeably. The sweet potato is full of minerals and vitamin A, and, true to its name, sugar. But it's best when the sugar is played against—the notorious marshmallow-topped candied sweets of childhood just don't do justice to the pleasures of this colorful food.

There are dozens of ways to make the sweet potato a treat instead of a mass of goo. But there's at least one currently chic thing I wouldn't do with them: They don't crisp up properly when they're deep-fried, so I pass on that; but, they mash as nicely as white potatoes, and unlike mashed white potatoes can be reheated nicely or transformed next day into a casserole. And it's easy to take a leaf from the Africans and cook them up with meat, greens, and other vegetables for a soup or stew with a difference. Sweet potatoes are rich, colorful, and only marginally sweet. Try them as if they were an entirely new vegetable.

SMALL PLATES

Grilled Pork Skewers on Beds of Sweet Potato

SERVES 8

3 large sweet potatoes
¼ pound butter
1 cup heavy cream
Salt and pepper to taste
½ cup grated Parmesan
    cheese
2 eggs, well beaten
2 pounds pork tenderloin, cut
    into 1½-inch chunks
3 large red bell peppers, cut
    into 1½-inch pieces

2 large red onions, cut into
    1½-inch pieces, 2 layers
    deep
4 large greening apples, cored
    and cut into 1½-inch
    pieces
4 cups good cider
4 garlic cloves, chopped
½ cup soy sauce

Preheat oven to 425° F.

Peel and quarter sweet potatoes. Boil until tender. Heat butter and cream until butter melts. Mash sweet potatoes, then whip in butter and cream. Add salt, pepper, and cheese, then fold in well-beaten eggs. Pipe in a closed spiral 4 inches in diameter onto each of eight 6-inch ovenproof plates. Fifteen minutes before serving time, put plates on cookie sheets and slip into oven.

String pork, peppers, onions, and apple pieces on 8 well-soaked 4-inch wooden skewers. Lay skewers in one layer in a roasting pan.

Boil cider and garlic in a nonreactive pan until cider is reduced by one half. Stir in soy sauce and pour over skewers. Let stand, rotating occasionally, for an hour or so. Grill over medium heat until pork is cooked through, about 5½ minutes to the side.

Push meat and vegetables off skewers in a semicircle onto each plate of hot baked mashed potato. Serve at once.

Savory Sweet Potato Soufflé

SERVES 8

2 large sweet potatoes
4 tablespoons butter
3 cups milk
1½ teaspoons salt
1 teaspoon black pepper
1 teaspoon ground cardamom
1 teaspoon ground coriander

4 egg yolks, beaten
8 egg whites
½ teaspoon cream of tartar
¼ cup clarified butter
2 cups fine-ground pistachio
    nuts

Preheat oven to 425° F.

Peel and quarter sweet potatoes and boil until tender. Mash. Heat butter and milk until butter is melted and milk almost scalded; beat into sweet potatoes with salt, pepper, cardamom, and coriander. Add beaten egg yolks slowly, beating all the while. Mixture should be the consistency of a medium white sauce. Beat egg whites in a large bowl with a balloon whisk until frothy. Add the cream of tartar and beat until the mixture forms stiff peaks. Stir a third of the whites into the cooled sweet potato mixture, then fold into remaining egg whites.

Grease eight 6-ounce soufflé dishes with clarified butter and dust with 1¼ cups of the pistachio nuts. Pile sweet potato mixture to just above the rims of the dishes and sprinkle with remaining pistachios.

Bake for 35 to 40 minutes, or until fully risen, puffy, and brown. Serve with the speed of light.

SALADS

✖

Sweet Potato Salad

SERVES 8

The nice thing about this dish is that it *isn't* white potato salad—it's a nice surprise to accompany pork, smoked or fresh, veal, or fowl.

4 large sweet potatoes	4 celery ribs
2 cups orange juice	2 large Ida Red or Rome
2 teaspoons grated orange	apples
zest	Salt and pepper to taste
2 cups seedless green grapes	3 cups sour cream
1 medium jicama	

Peel and halve sweet potatoes and boil until just tender. Pour orange juice and zest, stirred together, over potatoes and toss; chill.

When ready to serve, halve the green grapes and cut jicama, celery, and cored apples into medium dice. Dice drained sweet potatoes. Toss everything together with salt and pepper and bind lightly with sour cream.

Honeydew and Sweet Potato with Blueberry-Tarragon Dressing

SERVES 8

The density of the sweet potato and the lightness of the honeydew are the nice contrast here, with the colors of dark greens and pale blueberry dressing forming a happily odd background.

4 medium sweet potatoes
1 large honeydew melon
1 pint Blueberry-Tarragon
   Dressing (page 29)

1 bunch arugula
1 bunch watercress

Bake sweet potatoes in their skins until tender, about 1 hour at 400° F; chill. Cut chilled melon longtitudinally. Seed and peel. Cut in quarters and then into ¼-inch slices. Carefully peel sweet potatoes and cut into ¼-inch slices. On each of eight 10-inch plates, drift a pool of dressing. Alternate slices of melon and sweet potato on half the plate; arrange a tangle of arugula and watercress on the other half.

For a light but wonderful lunch, serve to 6 and add half a smoked chicken breast or a grilled fresh one to each plate.

SOUPS

✖

Sweet Potato, Mustard Green, and Chicken Soup

SERVES 8

Chicken is bland, mustard greens are peppery, and sweet potatoes are starchy-sweet. Good stuff.

2 ounces fresh ginger
2 curls orange zest
1 gallon good chicken stock
2 medium sweet potatoes, peeled and diced

8 chicken tenderloins, slivered
Salt and pepper to taste
1 bunch young mustard greens

Simmer slivered ginger and orange zest in chicken stock for about 45 minutes. Strain. Cook sweet potatoes in flavored stock until just tender. Add chicken slivers. Cook until chicken is just done, about 3 minutes. Season with salt and pepper.

Tear washed, stemmed greens into small pieces and place a good handful in each of eight large soup bowls. Ladle hot soup over greens and serve at once.

Sweet Tomato Soup with Sweet Potatoes and Sultanas

SERVES 8

2 medium sweet potatoes,
  peeled
2 cups Rhine wine
1 cup sultanas
8 large dead-ripe fresh
  tomatoes
2 large Bermuda or Vidalia
  onions

4 tablespoons butter
2 cinnamon sticks
½ cup brown sugar
½ teaspoon cayenne
½ teaspoon salt
2 cups cider

Cut sweet potatoes in medium dice and boil until just tender. Meanwhile, boil white wine and drop in sultanas. Remove from heat and let raisins soak.

As soon as sweet potatoes are tender, drain and pour white wine and raisins over them. Let stand at room temperature.

Peel tomatoes. Peel onions and dice. In a heavy nonreactive 1-gallon saucepan, sauté onions in butter until very limp, being careful not to brown. Chop tomatoes into onions, stir, add cinnamon sticks, and cook slowly until very mushy. Add sugar, cayenne, and salt and continue cooking for 10 minutes or so. Add the cider and continue cooking briefly, stirring. Strain through a chinoise or fine-mesh sieve. Reheat and stir in sweet potatoes and sultanas with the wine they soaked in. Serve at once.

MAIN COURSES

※

Fresh Ham with Sweet Potatoes, Dried and Fresh Fruit

SERVES 12

1 fresh ham, about 10 pounds
3 quarts orange juice
2 quarts Gewurtztraminer or
other spicy-sweet white
wine
6 large sweet potatoes
½ pound butter

1 pound dried apricots
1 pound dried peaches
1 pound dried pitted prunes
6 apples, Ida Red or Cortland
2 teaspoons salt
1 teaspoon pepper

Preheat oven to 400° F; bake the ham for 1½ hours, set on a rack well above a large roasting pan. In the last 30 minutes of cooking, baste with a mixture of 1 quart orange juice and 1 quart wine.

Meanwhile, peel and slice the sweet potatoes into cold water. Heat the remaining orange juice, wine, butter, and salt and pepper together almost to boiling and pour over dried fruit. Peel, core, and slice the apples. When the ham has been in the oven for an hour and a half, remove it and distribute the potatoes under the rack. Baste with the orange juice mixture and return to the oven at 425° F. When potatoes are just beginning to be tender (about 25 minutes), add dried fruit and apples to the pan. Baste ham with the mixture the fruit has been soaking in. Pour the rest of the mixture over the fruit.

Bake for another 30 minutes, or until a meat thermometer inserted at the thickest part of the leg reads 140° F, stirring potatoes and fruit together a couple of times, basting each time.

Serve ham in thin slices with generous spoonfuls of the sweet potato and fruit.

Ruby Chicken with Mashed Sweet Potatoes

SERVES 4

2 plump broiling or frying
   chickens, about 3 pounds
   each
Salt and pepper to taste
2 rosemary branches
4 bay leaves
2 ounces fresh ginger, cut in
   large dice

1 pound cranberries
2 cups sugar
2 ounces fresh ginger, grated
2 cups rich chicken stock
4 large sweet potatoes
1½ cups milk, scalded
¼ pound butter, melted
1 bunch watercress

Preheat oven to 425° F.

Season chickens with salt and pepper; remove body fat from cavities. Fill cavities with rosemary, bay leaves, and ginger. Truss chickens by tying the legs together and tucking the wing ends under and set on a rack with body fat on top. Roast for 45 minutes to 1 hour, or until a pricked thigh runs yellow.

While the chicken is roasting, rinse the cranberries and put in a 1-quart nonreactive pan with sugar, grated ginger, and a dash of salt. Simmer until the cranberries begin to break. Stir chicken stock into cranberries. Peel and quarter the sweet potatoes and boil until very tender; strain and mash and beat in the scalded milk and melted butter; season with salt and pepper.

Serve chicken slathered with cranberry sauce, with mashed sweet potatoes, and swags of watercress on the platter.

DESSERTS

Sweet Potato Pone

SERVES 8

This is very good stuff, but mysterious. I'd never heard of anything but *corn* pone until I was in my thirties—and corn pone is just a primitive form of corn bread, usually just corn and water, cooked in an iron skillet. Sweet potato pone is a pudding made with raw grated sweet potato, and is anything but primitive—it's full of good things, and I've seen dozens of variations on it. This one is extrapolated (by memory) from the recipe of a great Texas cook, Pearl House.

¼ pound butter	*1 cup coconut cream*
2 cups pecan pieces	*2 cups orange juice*
4 medium sweet potatoes	*2 cups heavy cream*
2 cups brown sugar	*1 cup toasted coconut*

Preheat oven to 350° F.

Melt the butter in a heavy skillet and add the pecans; toast lightly. Peel and grate raw sweet potatoes and toss in a 3-quart bowl with the pecans, the sugar, the coconut cream, the orange juice, and the heavy cream. Put in a buttered 3-quart casserole and bake for 1½ hours. Sprinkle with toasted coconut and serve warm with heavy cream.

Sweet Potato–Mango Pie

SERVES 8

4 medium sweet potatoes
1 large mango
Grated zest of 1 lime
3 cups milk
6 eggs
2 cups brown sugar
2 teaspoons ground nutmeg

1 teaspoon vanilla extract
Butter Pastry (page 53; use
  ½) for a one-crust pie
1 cup whipping cream
1 tablespoon confectioner's
  sugar
1 tablespoon Cointreau

Peel, halve, and boil sweet potatoes until very tender, about 30 minutes. Peel mango and strip flesh from the seed. Chop fine, being careful not to lose any juice. Mash mango, lime zest, and sweet potatoes together. Scald milk; beat eggs and add 1 cup of the hot milk, beating constantly. Whisk egg mixture into remaining milk. Add brown sugar, nutmeg, and vanilla. Stir into mango-sweet potato mixture.

Preheat oven to 350° F.

Roll out pastry and line a 10-inch pie pan. Pour in sweet potato custard and bake for 50 minutes, or until a knife inserted in the center comes out clean.

Whip cream until moderately thick, adding confectioner's sugar as you whip. Continue whipping until very thick and then stir in Cointreau. Serve as garnish.

OKRA AND
SOUTHERN GREENS

Greens and okra—they are a signature of southern food, of African-American food. I was raised on them, since my family hired a wonderful cook who lived with us for almost forty years, Rebecca Jackson Stringfellow. She could cook anything—she was trained by her own family and by my grandmother Lucy—but if left to herself (and we were very often content to do that) she cooked her own food, so I ate smothered pork chops, frizzled ham pieces, greens, okra, and corn bread through my whole childhood. I still have habits of eating that Sing taught me and that are shared by a lot of African-Americans, and a good many white people like me, who were raised by and among African-Americans. I love corn bread crumbled into collard greens with buttermilk; molasses more than any other syrup; okra in any form: pickled, fried, stewed with tomatoes; and long-cooked vegetables flavored with ham taste better to me than meat.

The greens I write about here are those specifically identified with the South and with black cooks, especially turnip greens, mustard greens, and collards, and those often eaten raw or wilted, poke and dandelion, that are hard to come by unless you order from a boutique produce man or live far enough out in the country to pick them. You'll find kale here, too, and some of the greens that turn up in Italian markets and are called by Italians "bitter"—they go very well with southern greens. I haven't limited myself to southern recipes, or even to traditional ones. One of the reasons to explore the cookery of greens is to illustrate their versatility, which is much greater than one would think. They are great by themselves, as a side dish; wilted or raw in salads; and as a freshening ingredient in soups and stews. But even if you limited yourself to basic ham-cooked greens with pepper vinegar, you'd be ahead of most Americans—they're not as aware as they should be of how fine a flavor greens add to ham, to fresh pork, to roast chicken.

Okra is a vegetable that suffers not only from misunderstanding, but also from a sort of skewed understanding. It's true that all those impolite and disgusting terms—*slimy* is probably the least distressing—that people apply to cooked okra really do apply, at least if okra isn't cooked properly. But if okra is cut and blanched before it's used in recipes, it's possible to turn it into a great vegetable and a thickening agent that takes the place of flour in a good many southern recipes.

Okra is one of our undoubted African culinary inheritances: The word for okra, gumbo, was brought straight to this country from Africa and became by extension the name of the stew that it thickened, the national dish of Cajun country in Louisiana, of which okra is a frequent though not invariable ingredient. One of the nicest things about okra is its shape—a flowerlike stem-end thinning to a point at the blossom end. It makes pickled okra a great addition to a relish plate or a salad bowl—odd and pretty.

With both okra and greens, availability can be a problem. Okra requires a long hot growing season, and so is largely a southern crop, though it's available in the North in the late summer, much as corn is. Greens are hardy and have a long season, but some of them, like collards and mustard and turnip greens, are considered regional or ethnic specialties and are hard to find outside the South or African-American communities elsewhere. As southern cookbooks have proliferated, though, we've begun to see greens turn up elsewhere, though not with any great reliability. Ask your supermarket manager to stock them.

SOME BASICS

Preparing and Cooking Greens

SERVES 8

This is the classic southern preparation of greens; collards are the longest to cook, with mustard and turnip coming in at a much quicker pace, but they are all eaten in the same way, with pepper vinegar as an accompaniment to meat, especially smoked pork. Lots of poor households had as their meat only the ham hocks or jowls cooked with the greens and black-eyed peas or field peas—the hocks or jowls were cooled, picked, and the meat was returned to the pot. The greens or peas were eaten as dinner, with corn bread or biscuits, and buttermilk, if there was a cow. For me, this is still the most satisfying of country meals.

3 ham hocks or two jowls
4 large bunches collard,
    mustard, or turnip greens

2 teaspoons black pepper
Salt to taste (adjust according
    to the saltiness of the ham)

Bring 1½ gallons (for mustard and turnip greens, 1 gallon) of water to a full boil with the ham hocks or jowls; boil for about 30 minutes before adding collard greens, 1 hour before adding mustard or turnip greens.

Wash the greens. The best method for washing greens is the same as that for washing spinach, although greens are much easier to get clean, being smoother than spinach: Fill a large pot with warm water and add a good handful of salt (the water should be salty to taste). Stem the greens. In the case of collard greens, you'll need to cut the heavy stem out of the biggest leaves, as you occasionally need to with spinach, and plunge them into the water. Let soak for 3 or 4

(continued)

minutes, then slosh them around thoroughly and lift out of the pot away from the water (never drain the water over the greens). Cut the greens into large but fork-manageable pieces and add them to the boiling water.

Cook collard greens for about 2 hours, mustard or turnip greens for 1 hour or less (very young mustard or turnip greens can be a quite short cook). At the very end of the cooking process, add the salt and pepper, being very careful not to oversalt. Remove the ham and cool. Pick the lean ham off the bones and return to the pot. Serve with pepper vinegar (2 tablespoons each cider vinegar and Tabasco) on the side or add to the pot. Greens should be drained only enough not to flood the plate—the liquid, or pot liquor, is as great a treat as the greens themselves.

Serve with ham, fried chicken, chicken-fried steak, or roast chicken.

Blanched Okra

1 pound good-size but tender okra pods	½ gallon water 2 teaspoons salt

Wash okra in hot water. Cut on the diagonal like French-cut green beans, or leave whole. Boil water with salt and blanch okra for 3 minutes. Drain and rinse with cold water. Proceed with whatever your recipe calls for.

SMALL PLATES

Fried Okra

SERVES 4

3 cups flour
1½ cups cornmeal
1 tablespoon cayenne
2 tablespoons black pepper
1 tablespoon salt
1 teaspoon dried oregano
1 teaspoon dried tarragon
1 pound large, fresh, firm
    okra pods, blanched (see
    preceding recipe)

3 cups buttermilk
4 cups soy oil or other
    neutral cooking oil
Tomato-Chili Yogurt Sauce
    (see following recipe)

Sift together flour and cornmeal. Season with the peppers, salt, and herbs. Roll blanched okra in the flour mixture, then drop in buttermilk, then roll in flour mixture again (be sure okra is thoroughly coated). Heat oil to 375° F and fry okra until golden brown. Serve plain, as an hors d'oeuvre, with the sauce for dipping, or as a first course, with the sauce spooned over.

Tomato-Chili Yogurt Sauce

MAKES 3 CUPS

There is in this sauce a suggestion of India, where okra is as popular as it is in the American south.

2 cups yogurt
2 perfectly ripe tomatoes,
  peeled and diced
¼ cup minced fresh jalapeños
½ small onion, diced fine
2 garlic cloves, minced
2 teaspoons dried ancho chili
  powder (page 151)

2 teaspoons ground cumin
1 teaspoon salt
2 teaspoons black pepper
2 heavy dashes of Tabasco
Juice and grated zest of 1
  lime

About half a day before you're to make the sauce, put yogurt in double cheesecloth and suspend in a strainer over a bowl. Set in a cool place.

Mix the tomatoes, jalapeños, onion, and garlic and let stand. Toast the chili powder and cumin seed in a small dry skillet over a medium flame. Toss the spices to prevent from burning; they will be toasted in 3 or 4 minutes. Let cool briefly and add with salt, pepper, Tabasco, lime juice, and zest to the tomato mixture.

Stir drained yogurt into the tomato mixture and toss lightly. Chill for about 1 hour.

Pickled Okra

MAKES 6 PINTS

We didn't have pickled okra when I was growing up—my memory is that it was a spinoff from the immensely popular dilly bean, the hot dill-pickled green bean that became a great favorite with cocktails (and sometimes *in* cocktails) in the fifties. The most common commercial version is from Texas, and perhaps my landsmen did not invent it—certainly it's not an *old* southern recipe, but by now it's found, along with the also-recent pickled jalapeños, on a lot of barbecue-restaurant relish trays. Certainly if you're disturbed by the gelatinousness of fresh okra, this is the answer.

2 pounds fresh okra pods, about 3 inches long	3 teaspoons mustard seed
6 garlic cloves	6 large dill sprigs, or 3 teaspoons dill seed
12 small hot red peppers, dried or fresh	3 cups white vinegar
3 teaspoons celery seed	¾ cup water
	¼ cup noniodized salt

The traditional method: Wash and stem the okra and stand them in 6 sterilized pint jars, alternating stem and pointed ends up for a snug fit. Include in each jar 1 garlic clove, cut in half, 2 hot-pepper pods, ½ teaspoon each celery and mustard seed, and a large sprig of fresh dill or ½ teaspoon dill seed. In a 1½-quart nonreactive saucepan, boil vinegar, water, and salt together for 5 minutes. Pour over okra, being sure to cover it completely. Seal the jars with new lids and store for at least 6 weeks to bring out the flavors. Serve chilled.

The icebox method: Wash and stem the okra and pack in a 2-quart pottery crock, layering with the garlic cloves cut in half, the peppers, celery seed, mustard seed, and dill. Boil vinegar, water, and salt together for 5 minutes and pour over okra. Weight the okra with a heavy plate and store in the refrigerator. The okra will be ready to eat in 1 week, and will keep for 6 or 8 weeks. It will not be quite as crisp as the pickles made the traditional way.

Serve as a cocktail snack or as a side dish with smoked pork, barbecue, or chicken.

Scalloped Tomatoes, Okra, and Green Chiles

SERVES 8

This is a slightly more formal version of the okra and tomatoes of my childhood—and though pickled okra may be a novel development in southern cooking, okra and tomatoes certainly aren't. This is the standard dinner dish, served with almost any main dish, and like a lot of southern vegetable dishes, relished almost more than any main dish. This makes a good light lunch or supper, with a spicy pilaf on the side.

1 medium onion, diced
2 celery ribs, diced
4 tablespoons butter
2 teaspoons salt
2 teaspoons black pepper
2 dashes of Tabasco
3 dashes of Worcestershire
  sauce
1 teaspoon oregano
2 cups sliced Blanched Okra
  (page 130)

4 cups strained, sliced canned
  plum tomatoes
    or
6 large ripe fresh tomatoes,
  peeled and sliced
1½ cups peeled, chopped
  green chiles
2 cups coarse saltine cracker
  crumbs
1½ cups grated pepper
  Monterey Jack cheese

Preheat oven to 400° F. In a large nonreactive skillet, sauté onion and celery in butter until almost soft. Add salt, pepper, Tabasco, Worcestershire sauce, and oregano and sauté for 3 or 4 minutes. Turn heat to high and add okra. Sauté for 5 minutes and add tomatoes and chiles and cook until most tomato liquid is absorbed. Turn into a 2-quart casserole and top with crumbs and cheese. Bake for 10 minutes, or until cheese is melted.

SOUPS

※

Pot Liquor with
Collard Greens, Potatoes, and Bacon

SERVES 8

My grandfather claimed to owe his life to pot liquor: When he was born, he was allergic to all forms of milk, even his mother's, and to save him he was given the pot liquor from collard greens in a baby bottle, on which he thrived until he was old enough to eat solid food. There's no reason to believe he wasn't being accurate, since collard greens are rich in calcium and vitamins D and A. With what protein was leeched from the ham the greens were cooked with, the pot liquor could just about have kept him alive. In any case, he lived to be eighty, dry and humorous and generally pleased with himself, and he never lost his taste for greens or pot liquor.

1 large bunch collard greens
1 gallon chicken stock
2 ham hocks
8 red-skinned potatoes
2 tablespoons cider vinegar

2 heavy dashes of Tabasco
Salt and pepper to taste
1 large red bell pepper
8 slices bacon, cooked crisp

Prepare greens for cooking (page 129), but cut into smaller pieces, about 1-inch square. Bring chicken stock to a boil with the ham hocks; add collard greens and simmer 2 hours. Add whole potatoes, vinegar, Tabasco, salt, and pepper. Cook until potatoes are tender.

At serving time, slice each potato into 8 wedges and arrange, one to a bowl, in a flower pattern. Ladle soup over potatoes, being generous with the greens, and garnish with slivered red pepper and crumbled bacon.

Cream of Turnip Soup with Turnip Greens

SERVES 8

1 gallon chicken stock
Greens from turnips, washed
  (page 129)
6 large white turnips
2 teaspoons nutmeg
½ teaspoon ground
  cardamom

Salt and pepper to taste
Grated zest of 1 lemon
2 cups heavy cream
2 teaspoons tiny julienne of
  lemon zest

Bring chicken stock to a boil. Cut turnip greens into ¼-inch strips and blanch for 1 minute in stock; reserve.

Wash and peel turnips and cut into quarters. Cook in stock until tender, about 30 minutes. Purée in a food processor or blender.

Heat turnip purée and thin to a pouring consistency with 2 cups of the chicken stock. Stir in nutmeg, cardamom, salt, pepper, and lemon zest. Add heavy cream and stir to blend. Garnish each bowl of soup with reserved turnip greens and minute curls of lemon zest.

SALADS

※

Wilted Mustard and Dandelion Greens with Goat Cheese and Toasted Pine Nuts

SERVES 4

This is a variation. The classic southern salad stops with the greens, bacon, and black pepper, occasionally adding a teaspoon of sugar. The cheese and pine nuts are awfully good, though, and certainly bring an old-fashioned salad up to date.

*1 bunch young mustard
  greens*
*1 bunch young dandelion
  greens (they must be
  picked before buds appear
  on the plants)*
*4 slices double-smoked
  bacon**

2 tablespoons bacon fat
*2 tablespoons balsamic
  vinegar*
½ cup toasted pine nuts
2 teaspoons black pepper
¼ pound Montrachet cheese

Wash the greens and shake dry. Cut off the stems and break greens into large pieces in a big bowl. Cut bacon in fine dice and heat bacon fat in a large cast-iron skillet; add bacon pieces and render over medium heat until they are brown; add vinegar, pine nuts, and pepper. Remove from heat and pour over greens, tossing and turning quickly; if there is any residue in the pan, use a handful of the greens held in tongs to wipe out the pan.

Divide greens among four plates and top with slices of Montrachet cheese.

* Double-smoked bacon is available at any specialty butcher; it comes in small, dark slabs and is very intense in flavor.

Young Mustard Greens, Vidalia Onions, and Red Peppers with Orange Vinaigrette

SERVES 4 TO 6

The first thing to learn about mustard greens is that they are the pepperiest of the peppery greens; remember, too, that their spice is unpredictable. It's wise to taste them before using, and if necessary lighten their flavor with another, milder green like watercress. They have a serious and exciting kick, and shouldn't be served to lighten the spice of a meal, but to heighten the mildness of it—they are the perfect foil for a black bean casserole, for instance, or chicken and dumplings.

2 bunches young mustard greens 1 Vidalia onion	1 large red bell pepper Orange Vinaigrette (see below)

Wash and dry greens and tear into bite-size pieces. Cut onion and red pepper into slivers and toss with greens; toss with vinaigrette.

Orange Vinaigrette

MAKES 1½ CUPS

⅓ cup red wine vinegar Zest and juice of 1 orange 2 teaspoons Dijon mustard Salt and pepper to taste	1 tablespoon chopped fresh thyme 1 cup mild olive oil

Whisk together vinegar, orange juice, zest, mustard, salt, pepper, and thyme; add olive oil in a slow stream, whisking constantly, to form an emulsion.

MAIN COURSES

Bean, Sausage, and Chicken Casserole on a Bed of Kale

SERVES 6 TO 8

This is a casserole I've done in dozens of variations, and I invite you to join me: It works with kidney or pinto beans, black beans, even lentils or yellow or green peas. You can use ham or prosciutto or any other smoked meat instead of (or in addition to) sausage, and duck or goose instead of chicken. It can be done without the greens, or with the greens stirred into the dish at the last moment, and of course, you can substitute collards or chard or mustard greens for the kale.

2 pounds dried Great
   Northern white beans
1 gallon chicken stock
½ cup olive oil
1 broiling chicken, cut at
   each joint as for frying
1 pound andouille or kielbasa
   or linguica sausage
2 carrots, diced
4 celery ribs, diced
1 large yellow onion, diced
6 garlic cloves, minced
2½ tablespoons chopped fresh
   thyme

2 tablespoons chopped fresh
   basil
1 tablespoon chopped fresh
   tarragon
1 lemon zest curl
2 bay leaves
2 ham hocks
2 tablespoons chopped parsley
3 heavy dashes of Tabasco
2 tablespoons vinegar
2 cups crushed canned
   tomatoes
2 bunches kale

Cover the beans with water and bring to a boil. Turn off the heat and let stand, covered, for 45 minutes. Return to heat and to the

(continued)

boil; turn down to a simmer. Replenish the water with chicken stock as needed. Cook for about 1 hour, or until beans are almost tender.

In a heavy skillet, heat the olive oil to very hot and sauté the chicken, seasoning with salt and pepper as you go. Cook only until chicken is brown and then remove from pan. Sauté sausage in one piece until brown. Remove and reserve.

Add carrots, celery, and onion to the pan the meat was browned in and sauté until vegetables begin to soften. Add garlic, thyme, basil, tarragon, lemon zest, and bay leaves; continue sautéing briefly. Deglaze the pan with a pint of the chicken stock and the tomatoes. Stir to combine and then add all to the beans, stirring to combine. Continue cooking at a simmer.

Bring remaining chicken stock to a boil with the ham hocks. Let simmer.

When beans are almost done, add sausage, cut into 2-inch slices, and chicken. Simmer until beans are tender almost to the point of dissolving and the chicken and sausage are done, about 30 minutes. (Test by piercing a thigh to see that it's not pink at the bone.) Add parsley and stir gently.

When chicken and sausage are almost done, add Tabasco and vinegar to simmering chicken stock and turn up to a boil. Add stemmed, washed kale, cut into ½-inch strips, and cook 10 to 15 minutes, until tender. Drain kale, reserving stock.

To serve, pile kale lightly on a deep platter. Remove lemon zest and bay leaves from beans and pile beans, chicken, and sausage on greens (if dish needs moisture, add some of the stock from the kale.) Serve at once, sprinkled with chopped parsley.

One Good Southern Stew

SERVES 6

½ gallon chicken stock
2 ham hocks
2 bay leaves
1 pound ground pork
1 tablespoon chopped fresh
   rosemary
2 teaspoons chopped fresh
   thyme
4 garlic cloves, minced
2 teaspoons ground allspice
2 teaspoons salt

2 teaspoons black pepper
1 teaspoon cayenne
2 tablespoons brown sugar
½ cup breadcrumbs, softened
   in ¼ cup milk
2 celery ribs
1 large red onion
1½ pounds sweet potatoes,
   peeled and cut into chunks
1 large bunch mustard greens

Simmer chicken stock with ham hocks and bay leaves for 1 hour. Preheat oven to 450° F.

Combine pork with rosemary, thyme, garlic, allspice, salt, pepper, cayenne, and brown sugar. Work in moistened breadcrumbs and shape into small meatballs—there should be about 1 dozen. Put meatballs on a sided cookie sheet and bake for about 20 minutes, until brown.

Slice the celery and onion into large dice. Using the fat rendered from the meatballs, sauté until lightly brown. Add celery, onion, and sweet potatoes to the simmering chicken stock. Cook until sweet potatoes are just done. Add the washed mustard greens, cut into 2-inch pieces, and the pork meatballs. Simmer until greens are just tender. Remove ham hocks and bay leaves and serve stew in soup bowls.

Greens-Stuffed Kentucky Ham with Red-Eye Gravy and Pecan-Stuffed Sweet Potatoes

SERVES 6

1 Kentucky ham, about 12
   pounds*
½ gallon chicken stock
6 sweet potatoes
3 large bunches collard
   greens
2 tablespoons cayenne
1 cup molasses
½ cup dry mustard
2 teaspoons nutmeg
2 tablespoons cider vinegar

½ pound butter
1 tablespoon sugar
2 teaspoons salt
2 cups pecan pieces
2 teaspoons black pepper
1 cup milk
1 cup grated provolone cheese
2 heavy dashes of Tabasco
2 tablespoons cider vinegar
2 cups white wine
5 cups strong coffee

Immerse ham in ½ gallon water and chicken stock and bring to a boil. Simmer for 1 hour, then cool in its liquid. Skin the ham, reserving the liquid and the skin.

Heat oven to 425° F and bake scrubbed sweet potatoes until tender, about 1 hour.

Bring ham liquid to a boil. Meanwhile, bone the skinned ham, laying out on a flat surface, inner side up. When ham liquid is at a boil, add ham bone and boil for 10 minutes; remove bone and skim fat from liquid. Add washed, stemmed, and chopped greens (see page 129) and boil for about 1½ hours.

While greens boil, rub the inside surface of the boned ham with 1 tablespoon of the cayenne. Mix molasses, mustard, nutmeg, and vinegar for ham glaze.

Melt 5 tablespoons of the butter and toss with remaining 1 table-spoon cayenne, sugar, and 1 teaspoon salt. Add the pecan pieces and toss until they are evenly coated with the butter mixture. Put them on a cookie sheet and put in the oven as you remove the sweet potatoes, turning the oven down to 325° F.

Cool the sweet potatoes briefly, then slit them at the top. Melt 6 tablespoons more of the butter, 2 teaspoons salt, 2 teaspoons black pepper, and milk together. Remove sweet potatoes from their skins and mash with the milk mixture until smooth and fluffy. Remove pecans from oven and toss with the mashed sweet potatoes. Return sweet potato mixture to the potato shells and top with remaining butter and provolone cheese. Set aside.

Strain greens, reserving liquid. Toss greens with Tabasco and vinegar and line ham with as much of the mixture as will comfortably fit (you are replacing the bone with greens). Skewer and tie the ham together around the greens, tucking in any that stray out. Set the ham skinned side up on a rack in a roasting pan. Score the ham and bake for 1 hour; remove from oven and spread thickly with glaze. Turn heat up to 400° F. Pour white wine and 1 cup of the pot liquor from the greens into the roasting pan and return to the oven to finish for 30 minutes.

Remove ham from the oven and replace with the sweet potatoes. Remove ham from the roasting pan and set aside in a warm place to rest before carving. To the liquid in the pan, add 1 cup of the ham glaze and the coffee. Correct the seasoning by adjusting the amount of pot liquor, coffee, and glaze. Simmer on top of the stove to marry the flavors, and skim off any excess ham fat. Remove sweet potatoes from oven—they should have been in about 15 minutes, long enough to melt the cheese.

Slice the ham and serve with extra greens, a sweet potato, and red-eye gravy on each plate.

* The best Kentucky ham is available from Colonel Newsome, 127 Highland Avenue, Princeton, KY 42445.

Okra Gumbo with Chicken, Andouille Sausage, and Shrimp

SERVES 8

In Louisiana, gumbos are categorized a number of ways—by main ingredients, by color of the roux, and by the thickening agent. The main thickening agents are okra and filé, the ground bark of the sassafras tree. Almost any ingredient will do for a gumbo, but I like best the ones that combine fowl, seafood, and smoked pork; in mixed-meat gumbos I like the roux as dark as I can comfortably make it, and I'm fonder of okra than of filé. My grandmother wouldn't put filé in the gumbo at all—she sprinkled the rice with it —and for some reason that began a prejudice in me. I like all the ingredients in the gumbo, not lurking on the rice. Hence this favorite.

2 cups flour
2 cups soy oil
½ pound tasso ham,* cut into
  ¼-inch cubes
1½ cups diced onion
1½ cups diced green pepper
1½ cups diced celery
2 bay leaves
2 tablespoons dried thyme
1 tablespoon dried basil
2 teaspoons dried oregano
4 garlic cloves, chopped
2 cups raw okra, cut into
  ¼-inch slices
1 chicken, cut at every joint,
  as for frying

2 pounds andouille sausage,
  cut into 1-inch slices
1 tablespoon salt
1½ tablespoons pepper
4 heavy dashes of Tabasco
¼ cup Worcestershire sauce
2 cups fine-chopped canned
  plum tomatoes and their
  juice
1 quart chicken stock
1 pound shrimp, peeled and
  deveined, tails on
¼ cup chopped fresh parsley
chopped scallions, for garnish

Whisk flour all at once into hot, almost smoking oil. Turn down heat to medium and whisk constantly until roux is very dark brown, almost black. Whisking must be constant, and to achieve a true dark brown, will need at least 30 minutes over medium heat. As soon as you are convinced that you have the darkest achievable brown, add all at once (have them ready in a single bowl) ham, onions, peppers, celery, herbs, and garlic. Be very careful at this point: The high heat of the roux combined with the liquid in the vegetables will create a cloud of steam—be sure to stand back from the pot as you add your bowl of ingredients.

Turn the flame down and stir to blend. Add okra at once and turn up heat again to medium. Stir well. Add chicken and sausage and stir everything together. Cook for 5 minutes, then add Tabasco, Worcestershire sauce, tomatoes, chicken stock, and salt and pepper. Simmer until chicken is done, about 20 minutes (do not overcook —chicken should be well cooked but still on the bone). Add shrimp and cook further just until shrimp is done, about 5 more minutes. Add parsley in last 5 minutes of cooking.

Serve at once over hot rice and sprinkle with chopped scallions.

* Tasso ham is the name for Louisiana spiced ham, which comes in bits and pieces, highly cured. It's used for flavoring almost any dish you'd use ham hocks in, and gives not only a smoked but a spicy flavor that's typically Cajun. Most specialty butchers can get it for you.

CHILES AND TOMATILLOS

I was raised in a part of the country where a good segment of the population counted chiles and tomatillos among their native foods —but the Tex-Mex restaurants of that period never served tomatillos, and the only chile was in the mild red chili sauce on the enchiladas. West of Texas in New Mexico, Hispanics and Anglos alike were feasting on green chili sauce with tomatillos, carne adobado with ancho chiles, chiles rellenos, and dozens of other dishes that included the full range of chile types and the mild, citrus pungency of tomatillos.

It wasn't until I found my way to Santa Fe that I realized how limited the Tex-Mex food I'd been raised on was, and how long the list of chiles and their uses. Now there's a supermarket chain in Texas called Fiesta that has great piles of fresh chiles in ten varieties, aisles and aisles of pickled and dried chiles, and tomatillos right beside tomatoes among the produce. I've discovered that there is a raft of traditional recipes that use chiles in all their different flavors and degrees of hotness, and that tomatillos are not, as I'd believed in my youth, green tomatoes, but a fruit all their own that is essential to green chile sauce, and that suggest a wide variety of uses that I would never have dreamed of.

This growth of knowledge from a narrow familiarity with an American ethnic kitchen to a wider intimacy with its dishes and raw materials is typical of the way American cookery is growing. I was raised with the notion that Tex-Mex food was something that was found in restaurants, and whose ingredients were limited to the one kind of cooking found in just those restaurants. Texas Red—the chili con carne my father made on Sundays—wasn't even an exception to this rule; because we made it, we didn't even consider it Mexican, but assumed it as our own, eaten with soda crackers and milk. The idea that the Hispanic kitchen might be much more complicated than the diluted version we were sold in Anglo-oriented restaurants never really occurred to us.

All that has changed in the last twenty years: Young chefs have gone out looking for regional and ethnic ingredients to create new dishes that would say "American" with new emphasis; supermarkets, to say nothing of specialty grocers and market gardeners, have discovered new products and a population of amateur cooks who want to try them; and travelers have developed an interest in a range of food that goes beyond canned water chestnuts, chili powder, and dried mushrooms to express regional and ethnic influences in this country.

So for an American cook to include a chapter on chiles and tomatillos in a book about the fruits of the American garden is no longer anomalous—these are the "new" American ingredients, used for decades by Hispanic-Americans, now pushed into the mainstrain by a broader definition of American cooking and American culture.

SOME BASICS

For years, the only chiles most Americans saw were the Italian peperoncini in vinegar, and the powdered anchos that make up chili powder. Then Mexican restaurants started putting lavish amounts of pickled jalapeños on nachos, and occasionally serving them in bowls as a relish; and New Mexican cooking began to show up beyond the borders of the state; and a lot of cookbooks introduced Americans to Mexican food from the original source. We're aware of dozens of kinds of chiles now; and tomatillos, which were unavailable outside the Southwest, are turning up in supermarkets.

I can't begin to tell you about all the chiles there are—they grow in bewildering profusion of size, color, and intensity of heat and flavor. I've confined myself to the handful of chiles I use most often, and that you are most likely to find in supermarkets; here's a short glossary of how they taste and what to do with them.

JALAPEÑO This is a short, fat, hot green pepper that usually comes fresh, in the produce section, or canned and pickled with other vegetables (usually labeled in Spanish "en escabeche"). It is full-flavored, greeny, and not as fiery hot as its reputation suggests. I like it minced fresh in soups and stews, and pickled on beans, nachos, and to eat out of hand.

POBLANO A slightly larger chile, and slightly milder, than the jalapeño, it is often used for green chile sauce.

ANCHO Short, fat, and dark red, it is the chief component of chili powder (along with cumin, coffee, garlic, and chocolate), and the most characteristic of the mild red chiles. It is not hot, but much richer than the sweet red pepper it slightly resembles. Along with cumin, it provides the dominant flavor of most Tex-Mex food, a flavor that has found its way across the country through Mexican fast-food chains and bars of all kinds.

NEW MEXICAN RISTRA Longer than the ancho, slightly hotter, its flavor is ancho-like, and it can be used in the same ways.

(continued)

SERRANO A small chile, usually dried when red, but sometimes seen fresh and green. Very hot. Good to add heat to dishes rich in other chile flavor.

CHILE PEQUIN Tiny and very hot, this chile is available fresh from bushes in yards from California to Texas, but is rarely seen outside a vinegar bottle elsewhere.

CHIPOTLES Not a type of pepper, but a type of treatment—dried or canned, these chiles, usually either jalapeños or serranos, are smoked as they're dried. The flavor is pronounced and a great addition to cooked or uncooked red chile sauces.

Making Dried Chiles into Chile Paste

This works best with large chiles—the smaller ones are too small to be turned into paste; you'll just be left with a collection of seeds and wet skin.

Stem and seed the chiles. Pour boiling water over dried chiles, to cover. Let stand until water has cooled enough to let the chiles be handled. Run through a fine sieve. Chop coarse or purée.

Making Your Own Chili Powder

MAKES ¾ CUP

The question of what to do with dried chiles has come up in most kitchens only in the last ten years—until then, most of us saw chiles only in the form of chili powder, which we put in chili con carne, and that was that. Now, with chiles available in beautiful profusion, we'd better learn how to deal with them.

There is really no good, full-flavored chili powder in cans: It is usually flat, often stale, and a bit dull. Making your own is easy enough and tastes wonderful.

12 dried ancho chiles
3 tablespoons ground cumin
1 tablespoon unsweetened
  cocoa powder

2 teaspoons triple-ground
  espresso coffee

Seed and stem the chiles and whiz them in the food processor bowl for at least 5 minutes, until they are reduced to a fine powder. Or use a small-bowled coffee grinder and whiz until they are reduced to a fine powder. Combine with the cumin, cocoa, and coffee. Use as you would any chili powder.

Any dried chile can be reduced to a powder this way; and used to flavor any preparation.

Roasting Fresh Chiles

Fresh chiles can be used by just slicing or mincing and adding directly to sauces or stews; but a great flavor is added by roasting and peeling the chiles; again, the bigger the chile, the more practical the process.

12 fresh chiles, poblanos,
*   serrano, jalapeño or other*

Put chiles directly on the high flame of a gas stove, or over a charcoal or gas grill. Let the chiles go dark, and turn until they're dark all over. Put them in a paper bag and seal. Let stand for 15 or 20 minutes, then remove them one at a time and scrape the skin away from the flesh, retaining the flesh. Don't worry if a bit of skin is left behind or if some of the flesh is slightly charred. Chop coarse or purée.

SMALL PLATES

Cheddar-Stuffed Deep-Fried Jalapeños

SERVES 4

Dennis Egan is the most efficient cook I've ever worked with—it's hard to see that he's moving at all, even when he's getting out a banquet for three hundred. He gave me this recipe, announcing that it marked the graduation of the New York palate from bland. His origins are in New England, so he and New York were vaulting together into the fiery.

16 large fresh or pickled jalapeños
2 cups grated sharp Cheddar cheese
1 tablespoon ground cumin
2 cups flour
1½ cups buttermilk
3 cups breadcrumbs
1 teaspoon dried oregano
1 teaspoon black pepper
1½ teaspoons salt
4 cups soy oil
Tomato-Chipotle Sauce (see following recipe)

Slit each jalapeño lengthwise along one side from tip to stem end and remove the seeds. Be careful to keep the body of the peppers intact. Toss Cheddar with cumin and stuff into jalapeños, pressing each slit side around the cheese (the cheese will bulge out).

Dip each pepper in flour, then in buttermilk, then in breadcrumbs mixed with oregano, black pepper, and salt. Be careful to cover each pepper completely, leaving no bit of pepper or cheese uncovered. (Any bit of uncovered pepper or cheese will let the hot oil boil the cheese out of the jalapeños.)

Heat soy oil to 375° F, or almost smoking, in an 8-inch skillet. Fry peppers 3 or 4 at a time until golden brown, about 1½ minutes each. Drain briefly on paper towels and serve at once with Tomato-Chipotle sauce.

Tomato-Chipotle Sauce

1 small green bell pepper
1 small onion
2 tablespoons soy oil
1 large garlic clove, minced
Salt and pepper to taste

2 cups canned tomatoes, fine-
  chopped, with juice
3 canned chipotle peppers,
  stemmed and fine-chopped

Fine-dice green pepper and onion and sauté in soy oil. Add minced garlic, salt, and pepper. Add tomatoes and chopped chipotles and simmer very briefly. Serve in ramekins or custard cups as a dipping sauce.

Green Corn Tamales with Tomatillo-Poblano Sauce

SERVES 6 AS A FIRST COURSE

Tamales are a rich enough treat with dried corn alone—with fresh corn and a good green chile sauce, they're as delicate as they are charming, wrapped up for each eater like a little gift package.

2 cups pork shoulder cubes
  (about ½ pound)
1 onion, chopped
1 large garlic clove, minced
2 cups chicken stock
2 poblano chiles, minced
6 ears fresh young corn

1 teaspoon salt
1 teaspoon black pepper
1 cup masa harina
6 corn husks
Tomatillo-Poblano Sauce (see
  following recipe)
1 cup chopped red bell pepper

Simmer pork shoulder, onion, and garlic in chicken stock for about 30 minutes, or until pork is tender to the point of falling apart and liquid is almost evaporated. Add chiles and cook until mixture is quite dry. Chop pork mixture very fine.

Strip corn from ears by splitting each row of kernels down the center with a sharp knife and then skiving (cutting close to the cob) the corn from the ear. Chop corn fine, being careful to save all juice. Sprinkle corn with salt, pepper, and masa harina.

Steam corn husks until soft, about 10 minutes. Spread warm moist husks out and spread corn mixture to a ¼-inch thickness in a rectangle at the center of each husk, reaching to within ¼ inch of the edges of the husk. Place 1 tablespoon of the pork at the center of the corn mixture, then fold the corn husk into a package, lengthwise first, and then from each end. Or tie the ends with string or a strip of husk.

Steam tamales for 30 minutes over boiling water.

Serve in the husk, to be unwrapped at table; sauce may be poured over or used for dipping. Sprinkle with chopped red pepper for color.

Tomatillo-Poblano Sauce

12 large tomatillos, cleaned
   of papery covering
4 poblano chiles
1 red onion
2 tablespoons soy oil
2 garlic cloves, minced

2 teaspoons ground cumin
1 teaspoon salt
1 teaspoon black pepper
Chicken stock or white wine
   as needed to moisten

Mince tomatillos, poblanos, and onion and sauté in soy oil until soft, taking care not to brown. Add garlic and sauté until soft; add cumin, salt, and pepper. If sauce is too dry, add ½ cup chicken stock or white wine to moisten.

Fiery Chicken Chilequiles

SERVES 4

A lot of chile-based dishes aren't hot; they're just rich with the taste of pepper. But this little number is very, very hot, enriched but not much lightened by the eggs. Be prepared!

2 tablespoons soy oil
1 onion, diced
2 poblano chiles, minced
2 serrano chiles, minced
4 canned or fresh green
    chiles, fine-chopped
1 large garlic clove, minced
2 teaspoons ground cumin

Salt and pepper to taste
2 skinned and boned chicken
    breasts, tenderloin
    removed, cut into strips
½ cup chicken stock
3 corn tortillas, cut into
    ¼-inch strips
6 eggs

Heat soy oil over medium flame and sauté onion, chiles, garlic, cumin, salt, and pepper. Add chicken strips and cook until just past alabaster. Add chicken stock and simmer until amost evaporated. Stir in tortillas and toss with chicken and chiles. Beat eggs until fluffy and stir into chicken and tortillas, tossing the mixture with a fork and scraping the sides of the pan to the center. Cook just long enough to blend the mixture and until the eggs are softly set. Serve as is or with a drizzle of Tomato-Chipotle Sauce (page 154).

SOUPS

Tortilla Soup

SERVES 8

This is a nicely complicated soup with a very simple base: The broth and the tortillas make it as down-to-earth as the staffs of life of Mexican food, beans and corn. The condiments, added to each bowl at table, deepen and enrich it.

1 gallon skimmed chicken
   stock
4 garlic cloves, chopped
1 tablespoon whole cumin
   seed
3 dried star anise
1 tablespoon salt
1 tablespoon black
   peppercorns, slightly
   crushed
6 corn tortillas, cut into
   ¼-inch strips and dried
   overnight

4 scallions, minced
4 large fresh jalapeños,
   minced
½ cup grated aged dry
   Monterey Jack cheese
½ cup coriander leaves
Lime slices
2 cups Ancho-Garlic
   Mayonnaise (see following
   recipe)

Simmer chicken stock for about 1 hour, until reduced by a third. Add garlic, cumin, anise, salt, and black pepper and simmer further for 30 minutes. Strain and ladle into bowls over handfuls of tortilla strips.

Serve with scallions, jalapeños, cheese, coriander leaves, and lime, to add at table, along with a dollop of the mayonnaise.

Ancho-Garlic Mayonnaise

I designed this to give extra richness to an already complicated soup
—but if you're home with a tortilla and a few shreds of chicken, try
warming the tortilla, spreading it with this mayo, and adding the
chicken. Roll it up and that's lunch. Or maybe that and two or three
more; I've never been able to stop with one.

2 tablespoons ancho chile
   paste (page 150)
2 large garlic cloves, minced
½ teaspoon salt

½ teaspoon black pepper
1 egg yolk
1 cup soy oil

Beat ancho paste, garlic, salt, and pepper together with the egg yolk.
Slowly add the oil, drop by drop, whisking all the time. As oil is
incorporated, pour a bit faster, ending with a slow thin stream.

Yellow Squash Soup with Green Chile Drizzle

SERVES 8

Mexican cooking makes great use of squash, but that tradition hasn't found its way into many restaurants. This is a soup of mine with a chile addition that transforms it into something not of the North.

2 large onions, diced
8 cups quartered and sliced
   yellow squash
¼ cup soy oil
3 large garlic cloves, minced

1 tablespoon salt
1 tablespoon black pepper
2 quarts chicken stock
Green Chile Drizzle (see
   following recipe)

In a 1-gallon saucepan over a low flame, sauté onion and squash in soy oil until very soft and beginning to turn beige, about 45 minutes; you will have to stir almost constantly. Add garlic, salt, and pepper and cook 20 minutes longer. Purée in a food processor. Return to pan and stir in chicken stock; simmer for about 30 minutes, until all flavors are married. Strain through a chinoise or fine-mesh sieve and reheat.

Serve soup with a drizzle of green chile purée on top; sprinkle with bright red New Mexican chili powder.

Green Chile Drizzle

2 cups green chiles, canned or
    fresh, peeled and seeded
1 onion, diced
2 tablespoons soy oil
2 teaspoons ground cumin

2 tablespoons chopped fresh
    coriander
1 teaspoon salt
1 teaspoon black pepper

Sauté green chiles and onion in soy oil with cumin, coriander, salt
and pepper, until onion is very soft and chiles are almost liquid.
Purée until very smooth.

SALADS

◈

Mixed Greens with
Chile Vinaigrette

The dark flavor of the anchos makes this a lovely salad with grilled meat; an anchor, too, for the lightness of grilled or poached fish.

MIXED GREENS
*romaine, chicory, mustard
greens, arugula, oak leaf
lettuce*

CHILE VINAIGRETTE
*⅓ cup red wine vinegar
1 tablespoon Dijon mustard
2 tablespoons ancho chile
paste (page 150)*

*Salt and pepper to taste
1 cup light olive oil
1 tablespoon chopped fresh
coriander*

Stir mustard, vinegar, chile paste, salt, and pepper together. Whisk in oil in a small drizzle to emulsify. Stir in coriander. Use 1 tablespoon of dressing to toss with each 2 cups of mixed greens.

Oranges and Red Peppers
with Pepper Vinegar

SERVES 4

Hot, sweet, and sour is a combination of flavors that intrigues me more and more as I go on cooking. It is the ultimate refresher after a rich main course, and is satisfying in the absence of oil.

60 chiles pequins (also called
*   bird peppers)*
1 quart cider vinegar

6 navel oranges
2 large red bell peppers
2 bunches watercress

At least 2 days before serving, pierce each chile pequin with a needle and put in a quart bottle—or divide between two pint cruets. Pour vinegar over the peppers and steep. It will keep for at least 6 months.

Using a vegetable peeler, slice strips of orange peel from one of the oranges, being careful not to shave off any of the white pith. Cut into tiny julienne.

Peel and section the oranges and toss with the julienned zest. Cut the peppers into strips and toss with the oranges and a tablespoon or so of pepper vinegar. Serve on a tangle of watercress.

MAIN COURSES

Mexican Flag Enchiladas

(Chicken Enchiladas with Green Sauce, Beef Enchiladas with Red Sauce, and Sour Cream)

SERVES 4

This is simple, highly presentational dish that is very good to eat and very easy to make. The fun is in the contrast of color as well as flavor—the light brightness of green chile and the dark richness of red chile, relieved by the whiteness of the sour cream—all in imitation of the colors of the Mexican flag. A nice dish for Cinco de Mayo, complete with piñatas, firecrackers, and a nice rousing speech about patriotic death.

THE CHICKEN ENCHILADAS

4 corn tortillas
1 cup poached, picked chicken pieces
Salt and pepper to taste
1 cup grated white Monterey Jack cheese
1 cup toasted almond slivers

GREEN SAUCE

2 onions, diced
¼ cup soy oil
2 cups peeled, diced green chiles, canned or fresh
1 cup diced tomatillos
1 tablespoon ground cumin
2 tablespoons chopped fresh coriander
2 garlic cloves, chopped
1 teaspoon salt
1 teaspoon black pepper
2 cups chicken stock
1 tablespoon cornstarch

(continued)

For the sauce, sauté onion in oil until very soft; add chiles and tomatillos and sauté until soft and well blended. Add salt and pepper, cumin, garlic, and coriander. Simmer briefly, then add stock and cook down almost a third. Dissolve cornstarch in water and stir into sauce. Simmer for 5 minutes, or until cornstarch is incorporated and becomes translucent.

To assemble, in each corn tortilla, roll ¼ cup of the chicken seasoned with salt and pepper and ⅛ cup of the cheese. Lay enchiladas side by side on a heatproof platter and mask with the green sauce. Sprinkle with almond slivers.

THE BEEF ENCHILADAS

½ pound trimmed chuck
1 ounce fat from chuck
1 onion
1 tablespoon ground cumin
1 tablespoon ancho chili powder (page 151)
2 garlic cloves

Salt and pepper to taste
½ cup fine-chopped canned tomatoes
12 cups beef stock
4 corn tortillas
2½ cups grated Cheddar cheese

RED SAUCE

1 onion
¼ cup soy oil
¼ cup flour
Salt and pepper to taste
2 garlic cloves, minced
2 cups ancho chile paste (page 150)

2 teaspoons ground cumin
1 teaspoon unsweetened cocoa powder
2 cups beef stock

Heat beef fat in a heavy skillet until it has browned and rendered its fat. Remove browned piece and add the chuck, cut into 2 x ½-inch strips. Brown well and add the onion, cumin, chili powder, garlic, salt, and pepper and sauté until onion is translucent. Add tomatoes and beef stock and simmer until beef begins to shred, about 40 minutes. Continue cooking, over a very low flame, until liquid is almost evaporated.

For the sauce, dice onion and sauté in soy oil until translucent. Add flour, salt, and pepper and sauté until flour begins to turn beige, about 5 minutes. Add garlic, ancho paste, cumin, and cocoa powder. Blend carefully. Scrape into the bowl of a food processor and whiz until completely puréed. Return to pan and add beef stock. Reheat.

To assemble the enchiladas, roll a quarter of the beef in each corn tortilla with ¼ cup sharp Cheddar, salt and pepper. Lay beside the chicken enchiladas on the heatproof platter, leaving a couple of inches between the two sets. Mask enchiladas with red sauce and top with the remaining cheese. Slip into a 400° F oven until the cheese melts inside the enchiladas. Spoon a wide strip of sour cream between red and green enchiladas, letting it overlap on both sides. Decorate the plate with shredded iceberg lettuce and coriander leaves.

Grilled Kingfish and Green Chiles with Avocado Salsa

SERVES 4

This is fresh as a daisy and owes its complex salsa to John Bennett, the great Oklahoma chef who will put anything together with anything, as long as it tastes good. That he is so sure of what tastes good is what makes him such a great chef.

4 kingfish fillets, about 7 ounces each	Salt and pepper
6 large fresh green chiles	1 tablespoon ground cumin
2 cups olive oil	Avocado Salsa (see below)

Dip chiles in oil and grill for 4 minutes, turning once. Put chiles in a paper bag and seal.

Dip kingfish fillets in olive oil and grill for 4 to 5 minutes on each side, sprinkling with salt and pepper. As the fish comes off the grill, sprinkle each fillet lightly with ground cumin.

While fish is grilling, peel and seed the chiles and cut into strips. Serve the fish topped with the pepper strips and salsa beside it.

Avocado Salsa

2 firm avocados, fine-diced	2 large slices carrots from jalapeño jar, minced
2 blood oranges, sectioned and diced	2 tablespoons balsamic vinegar
Grated zest of 1 blood orange	Juice and grated zest of 1 lime
¼ large jicama, fine-diced	
2 pickled jalapeños, seeded and minced	

Toss all ingredients together.

Grilled New York Strip Steak and Black-Eyed Pea Relish with Chipotle Peppers

SERVES 4

If you are still an unapologetic beef eater, one of the tricks to having your red meat and keeping your health is to surround the main dish with low-fat, high-flavor dishes that won't further burden the system. Here, the relish is high-fiber and low-fat and complements the meat perfectly. End with melon and you will have done yourself a minimum of harm for a maximum of lovely taste.

4 New York strip steaks, 8
   ounces each, trimmed of
   fat and gristle
1 cup light olive oil

SLATHER
4 tablespoons soft butter
2 teaspoons toasted cumin
2 garlic cloves, mashed
Juice and grated zest of 1
   lime

Salt and pepper to taste
2 cups Black-Eyed Pea Relish
   (see following recipe)
Chiffonade of romaine lettuce

1 tablespoon tomato paste
Salt and pepper to taste

Work slather ingredients together thoroughly and set in refrigerator while steaks are cooking. Dip steaks in olive oil and season with salt and pepper. Grill for 5 minutes a side, to medium rare. Slather each steak with the butter mixture and serve on a bed of lettuce with sliced tomatoes and generous dollops of the relish.

Black-Eyed Pea Relish
with Chipotles

The earthy taste of black-eyed peas and the smokiness of chipotles are perfect together here—remember, though, that you'll need to cook this about eight hours before you grill the steaks.

2 pounds dried black-eyed
  peas
2 bay leaves
¼ large jicama, diced
3 celery ribs, diced
1 red onion, diced

1 red bell pepper, diced
2 garlic cloves, minced
4 chipotle peppers, canned in
  tomato sauce, with sauce
¼ cup red wine vinegar
Salt and pepper to taste

Cover peas with water and bring to a boil. Turn off flame and let stand for 45 minutes. Add bay leaves and turn the heat on again. Cook for about 1 hour longer, until the peas are tender and beginning to fall apart. Cool.

Stir jicama, celery, onion, pepper, and garlic into the peas. Season with salt and pepper, then add chopped chipotles and vinegar.

DESSERTS

※

Lemon-Orange Cream Tarts with Jalapeño-Jelly Glaze

MAKES 1 DOZEN TARTS

2 cups milk
5 egg yolks
⅔ cup sugar
Juice and zest of 1 lemon
Juice and zest of 1 orange
¼ cup flour
1 double-crust recipe plain
    Butter Pastry (page 53)

1 jar (8 ounces) jalapeño and
    sweet red pepper jelly,
    melted
Orange and lemon slices and
    fresh jalapeño slivers for
    garnish

Scald the milk in a 1-quart saucepan. Beat together the yolks, sugar, and citrus zests and juices. Add the flour, sprinkling it on the surface of the yolks and whisking to incorporate. Add the scalded milk gradually, stirring until well combined. Cook over low heat, stirring vigorously, until the cream comes close to the boiling point. Strain through a fine sieve.

Cut 5-inch rounds out of rolled pastry and fit into 4-inch tart shells. Line with foil and weight with beans or rice. Bake about 10 minutes at 400° F, watching like a hawk to keep them from burning. Fill tart shells to within ¼ inch of the top with pastry cream, then drizzle with a layer of melted jelly. Garnish with paper-thin orange and lemon slices and thin slivers of fresh jalapeño.

Tomatillo Jam Turnovers

MAKES 1 DOZEN TURNOVERS

This dessert demonstrates one of the nicest qualities of the tomatillo —its light citrus flavor, perfect for complementing the suavity of papaya.

4 cups tomatillos, peeled
1 cup water
2 cups brown sugar
Cookie Pastry Dough (see
   following recipe)

2 large papayas, peeled,
   seeded, and sliced

Chop peeled tomatillos and simmer with water until tender to the point of mushiness, 45 minutes to an hour. Add sugar and simmer until reduced to jam texture.

On a floured board, roll out pastry to ⅛-inch thickness and cut into 5-inch rounds. Put a tablespoon of the tomatillo mixture in the center of each round and fold in half, securing the edges with the tines of a fork. Bake at 400° F for about 10 minutes, until golden brown.

Serve warm with papaya slices.

Cookie Pastry Dough

2 cups flour
¼ pound plus 4 tablespoons
    soft unsalted butter
½ cup sugar

2 eggs
½ teaspoon salt
Grated rind of 1 lemon

Put all ingredients into the bowl of a food processor and run on and off for a few turns, or until ingredients are just blended. If the dough is too dry, add a splash of ice water. Roll into a ball and chill for 30 minutes.

JICAMA, JERUSALEM ARTICHOKES, AND SUGAR SNAP PEAS

⋇

Almost every fruit and vegetable in this book has by now found its way into most American supermarkets—even chiles, which until recently were downright exotic, are sitting right there next to the sweet green peppers. But these three are still a bit hard to find, in spite of a California effort to call the Jerusalem artichoke a "sunchoke" and sell it for salads.

Jicama is a big ugly watery root that has been common in the southwestern United States and Mexico for years. It is crunchier than celery, high in fiber, and low in calories and fat. It makes a wonderful palate-clearer after the hot richness of Mexican food or a complement to the light grilled things we're eating so much of right now. Good specialty greengrocers have it, and supermarkets are beginning to carry it as well.

The Jerusalem artichoke has been around for a long time, and has no relationship to the artichoke. It's a small, homely root, starchier than the jicama and almost as crunchy. Its starch content makes it a good vegetable for creaming or sautéing as a change from potatoes and rice; cooked, it has something of the texture of salsify, but unlike salsify, it has a distinct and satisfying flavor.

Sugar snap peas are a new hybrid—they pop up in early summer every year lately, but not everywhere and usually not for very long. Get them when you can, though, because they're wonderful—an edible-pod pea that has some succulent peas lurking inside. Cook them lightly if at all; they are the perfect raw vegetable for a dip.

SMALL PLATES

✖

Sugar Snap Peas Plain

SERVES 4 AS A FIRST COURSE,
6 AS A SIDE DISH

Sugar snaps, like asparagus and new corn and vine-ripened tomatoes, deserve a special place on the menu while they're newly available. Make a first course of these, with an absolute minimum of
dressing, and serve a glass of flinty Chardonnay with them, as a foil
for their perfectly fresh vegetable sweetness.

1 pound sugar snap peas
4 tablespoons butter, melted

1 teaspoon salt
1 teaspoon pepper

Bring 3 quarts of water to a boil. Remove stems and any strings
from the peas. Plunge the peas into the boiling water for 1 minute.
Drain and toss with melted butter, salt, and pepper. Serve at once as
a first course or as a side dish.

Jerusalem Artichokes and Leeks Parmesan

SERVES 4 AS A LIGHT LUNCHEON DISH, 6 AS A FIRST COURSE

The slightly sweet starchiness of the sunchokes and the grassy onion taste of the leeks make a perfect combination.

3 cups chicken stock	2 cups half-and-half
8 medium Jerusalem artichokes	1 teaspoon salt
	½ teaspoon black pepper
4 large leeks	2 heavy dashes of Tabasco
4 tablespoons butter	1 cup freshly grated
¼ cup flour	Parmesan cheese

Bring chicken stock to a boil. While it comes to a boil, peel and slice Jerusalem artichokes lengthwise into about 5 slices each, and put in a quart of water acidulated with half a lemon. Trim and halve leeks lengthwise and soak in salted water. After a 30-minute soak, wash leeks thoroughly and return to salted water until ready to cook.

When chicken stock comes to a boil, simmer artichoke slices and leeks for about 20 minutes, or until just tender. Drain, reserving stock, and alternate rows of overlapping artichoke slices with leeks on an ovenproof platter. Set aside in a warm place.

Melt butter and whisk in flour. Cook for 7 or 8 minutes over a medium flame, whisking constantly, until flour is thoroughly cooked and roux is beige. Bring 1½ cups of reserved stock and 1½ cups of half-and-half to a simmer and add all at once to hot roux. Whisk, and add salt, pepper, and Tabasco. Whisk in ⅔ cup Parmesan cheese. Stir until cheese melts. Mask artichokes and leeks with sauce, sprinkle with remainder of Parmesan cheese and bake until cheese browns and sauce bubbles, about 20 minutes. Serve at once.

If you'd like this dish to be purely vegetarian, poach the vegetables in a mixture of white wine and water and replace the stock for the sauce with another 1½ cups half-and-half. Use an extra ⅓ cup cheese in the sauce.

Jicama in Lime Cream
on Papaya Slices

SERVES 4

The crunchy jicama opposite the smooth sweet papaya, the lime good with both, the cream marrying all, and the whole light as a feather.

1 medium jicama	½ teaspoon salt
2 cups heavy cream	1 heavy dash of Tabasco
Juice and grated zest of 2 limes	1 large papaya
	1 lime, for garnish

Peel jicama (this will not be easy; jicama is big and hard—the easiest way is to halve the root, lay it flat side down, and shave the peel away). Slice ¼ inch thick and cut into 1-inch julienne.

In a small nonreactive saucepan, boil cream until reduced by half, about 20 minutes. Add lime juice and zest, salt, and Tabasco. Cool slightly and toss jicama with cream-lime mixture. Chill briefly.

Halve papaya and remove seeds. Peel and slice into 4 slices per quarter and sprinkle with lime juice. Lay 4 slices of papaya in a fan on each of four glass plates. Top with jicama in cream. Garnish with lime-slice curls.

SALADS

Jerusalem Waldorf

SERVES 6

6 medium Jerusalem
    artichokes
4 apples, Jonathan, winesap,
    or Ida Red
6 large pitted dates
2 celery ribs
2 cups black walnut pieces

½ cup Homemade
    Mayonnaise (see page
    103)
½ cup yogurt
2 tablespoons honey
½ head romaine
Chopped parsley, for garnish

Bring 4 cups of water to a boil. Peel artichokes and cut into ½-inch chunks. Blanch for 3 to 5 minutes, or until just tender. Plunge into ice water. Core and cut unpeeled apples into ½-inch chunks. Cut dates into 3 pieces each. Dice celery. Drain artichokes and toss with apples, dates, celery, and walnuts. Mix mayonnaise, yogurt, and honey. Toss with fruits and nuts.

Cut romaine into fine chiffonade. Pile on each of six plates and mound salad on lettuce. Garnish with chopped parsley.

Jicama-Cucumber-Melon-Orange Salad

SERVES 4 TO 6

This recipe was inspired by one of the most inspired restaurants in the country—the Frontera Grill in Chicago, run by Rick and Deann Bayless. Their food has the dark, sometimes murky richness of old Mexico, and a salad much like this one doubled as dessert for me one night. The watery crunchiness of the cucumber and jicama and the light sweetness of the orange make it the perfect foil for rich food.

2 limes	2 celery ribs
1 large jicama	4 yellow plum tomatoes
4 small cucumbers	½ romaine heart
4 navel oranges	½ bunch coriander
½ large honeydew melon	

Halve the limes and squeeze into a quart of ice water. Peel jicama, slice into 1 x ⅛-inch julienne, and plunge into lime water. Refrigerate.

Peel cucumbers and cut into small dice. Peel and section oranges and halve sections. Peel and seed melon and cut into ½-inch chunks. Pull strings from celery and dice small. Peel plum tomatoes and dice small.

Cut romaine into fine chiffonade and arrange on a platter. Arrange a mound of jicama in the center of the platter, like sticks in a game of pick-up-sticks. Surround with radiating circles of cucumber, oranges, celery, and tomatoes, from inside out. Garnish with coriander leaves.

To serve, toss everything together and mound on glass or bright-colored plates. Do not dress.

MAIN COURSES

※

Chicken Cutlets with Onion Sauce and Sugar Snaps

SERVES 4

Simple mildness with a great marriage of flavors: chicken, almond, onions, and sugar snaps. Unemphatic but memorable.

4 boneless, skinless chicken breasts, tenderloins stripped	2 onions
	2 cups chicken stock
	1 teaspoon nutmeg
4 cups peeled almonds	1 teaspoon salt
1 teaspoon cayenne	1 teaspoon pepper
1½ teaspoons salt	¼ pound butter
2 eggs	1 pound Sugar Snap Peas
1 cup milk	Plain (page 174)

Pound the chicken breasts between pieces of plastic wrap to ¼-inch thickness. Grind almonds to a fine powder in the bowl of a food processor (be sure to stop short of a paste). Toss ground almonds with cayenne and salt. Beat eggs and milk together. Dice onions and simmer in chicken stock until onions are very tender; add nutmeg, salt, and pepper. Purée in food processor. Add more stock, if necessary, to achieve pouring consistency.

Dip chicken breasts in flour, then in egg mixture, then in almond dust. In a heavy skillet, melt butter and let the foam die down. Brown chicken breasts on both sides over medium heat; turn heat down and cook just until chicken is done through, about 5 minutes. Turn, if necessary, to prevent burning. Do not overcook; chicken should be just past alabaster at the center.

Serve with onion sauce and cooked sugar snap peas.

Poached Veal Shoulder with Poached Vegetables

SERVES 10

1 shoulder of veal, about 4 pounds
3 tablespoons savory leaves
3 tablespoons marjoram leaves
3 tablespoons Italian parsley leaves
1 tablespoon salt
1 tablespoon pepper
2 washed anchovy fillets
¼ cup virgin olive oil

Chicken or white veal stock to cover
2 bay leaves
1 lemon zest curl
20 cracked peppercorns
10 baby carrots
10 baby turnips
10 small mushrooms
10 baby summer squash
20 sugar snap peas
10 Jerusalem artichokes

Bone and butterfly the veal shoulder, cutting through thick pieces of meat and reducing it as far as possible to one thickness. Lay the meat out on a board, trimming all excess fat. Chop herbs, salt, pepper, anchovies, and olive oil together and line the inside of the shoulder. Roll and tie. Bring stock to a boil with bay leaves, lemon zest, and peppercorns. Lower the shoulder into it, lower flame, and poach at a simmer, covered, until veal is done (just pinky alabaster at the center), about 1½ hours.

While veal is cooking, prepare vegetables for blanching: Remove all but ½ inch of top of carrots and turnips, trim mushroom stems, and stem and string peas. Peel and turn artichokes so that they're the same size as the mushrooms.

Remove veal to a warm place to stand. Strain and skim the stock. Return to a boil and blanch the carrots, turnips, and artichokes for 3 minutes, the other vegetables for 1 minute.

Turn up heat under stock and boil quickly to reduce by half. Slice shoulder, arrange slices to overlap, and then arrange each vegetable in a bunch around the meat. Correct stock for seasoning and spoon over meat.

SUMMER VARIATION

Cook shoulder as above; cook vegetables and refresh in ice water. Chill vegetables and shoulder.

Reduce stock as above, then clarify. For ½ gallon of stock, use 2 egg whites, 2 crushed eggshells, and ½ pound lean ground beef. Stir together whites, shells, and beef and put in a pot with the room-temperature stock. Bring stock to a *very* slow simmer and let cook —do not touch—for about 30 minutes. The beef and eggs will rise to the top of the stock to form a kind of raft, which will attract the solid particles in the stock. When the 30 minutes are up, pull aside the raft. If the stock below it is relatively clear and you can see heavy particles attaching to the bottom of the raft, the stock has clarified. Strain carefully through a sieve lined with a double thickness of cheesecloth.

Add 1 tablespoon gelatin, softened in ice water, for every quart of stock. Pour into a sided cookie sheet and chill for at least 1 hour. When veal is quite cold, serve with the vegetables as above; cut the aspic into diamonds and strew them between the vegetables, around the shoulder.

Serve with Homemade Mayonnaise (page 103) laced with puréed parsley.

AFTERWORD

IT IS POSSIBLE that I'm the most omnivorous person in the United States; certainly I believe that it's our human willingness as a species to eat anything that's edible that helps make us a dominant species —it's a great advantage not to be a picky eater. I go through life with my mouth open, ready for anything that tastes good. And it's no surprise that the native products of the country we live in taste very, very good.

What's been pleasurable about putting this book together is that the raw ingredients were there, ready to hand, suggestive of as many good things as I already knew—I found myself moving from traditional recipes to new ones to invented ones without a pause, drawn by the qualities of the foods themselves. That's the trick in any national kitchen—to find the characteristic materials and roam around among them, settling down to what they are really like and cooking from where they are.

I was born here, and that helps: Like every other American, I have a sense of where these ingredients have been in our past, how they're used now, and what we can do with them in the future. Often we just don't do enough, taking for granted what we have and relegating it to a corner of our consciousness. Our own abundance needs better treatment. Spending a year tasting the tartness of cranberries, the suave sweetness of blueberries, and the deep starchiness of pumpkin and sweet potato has given me that sense of the inexhaustible that is true to the food we were born to; my mouth is still tingling. I hope yours will be, too.

INDEX